BASIC SALESMANSHIP

LEARN & APPLY

RAJENDRA CHANDORKAR

Copyright © Rajendra Chandorkar
All Rights Reserved.

This book has been published with all efforts taken to make the material error-free after the consent of the author. However, the author and the publisher do not assume and hereby disclaim any liability to any party for any loss, damage, or disruption caused by errors or omissions, whether such errors or omissions result from negligence, accident, or any other cause.

While every effort has been made to avoid any mistake or omission, this publication is being sold on the condition and understanding that neither the author nor the publishers or printers would be liable in any manner to any person by reason of any mistake or omission in this publication or for any action taken or omitted to be taken or advice rendered or accepted on the basis of this work. For any defect in printing or binding the publishers will be liable only to replace the defective copy by another copy of this work then available.

This book is dedicated to all stakeholders in the process of sales.

Contents

Foreword

This book is for those innocent, naïve, young people who venture in the profession of sales as a last resort.They may be preparing for some exams and are doing sales jobs as a temporary assignment.

People with a one- or two-years stint in this gruelling field start wondering whether they are in a proper field or they should change, before the sad end sets in. Such people would find this book as a practical guide for their problems.

The language is as easy as it can be.

There are many unanswered questions in the young and old minds of the sales fraternity. A sincere effort is made to answer such queries. However, each person, products, organization, culture has its own advantages and shortcomings. Each customer is different and needs special attention, so one has to be slightly more involved and ready to stretch more than in any other field in the life. **"Sales is a process of today."** You cannot live in the past glory and enjoy the future projections. Those who understand this simple rule and try to be in today are somehow successful, they may even enjoy their stints, they may have excellent rapport with customers, dealers and the organization they work for. For others, every day is a *test*, every week is an *ordeal* and every month is an unforgiving *ongoing process* which only the salesman in the field understands.

***

Why this book?

In the formal management education, I never realised that I would have to unlearn many things which I was then learning with a lot of effort, money, and other resources. Yes, you can add exertion also. Then Philip Kotler was the last word in sales and marketing and even today he alone rules supreme. Any serious reader should get his queries answered if he reads it with some patience. His book deals mainly with classical marketing problems and dogmas which Indians find slightly alien. There are many other books for those who are willing and ready to put in some time.

After about forty years in sales and marketing as well as training, I thought I should share my experiences in simple language to those who are thrown to wolves without any real training. I hesitated before I shared my desire with my friends, about writing a book, they were not sure as to why. One of them was forthright and asked me 'Why this Book'? so I thought seriously and I explain as below.

The first reason to write this book is to provide answers to some of the doubts in the minds of those who choose to be sales and marketing professionals, with a stress on the practical aspects of the process.

Secondly, this book may serve the purpose of an initial "On the Job" training kit. This is a book for the starters in the field as well as for those who have spent some uneasy time in the field, somehow by fluke achieved some results but presently in a state of amazed inertia and in a constant mental debate whether they are in the right field or not.

Thirdly for those who have a formal training in management, but suddenly are extremely uncomfortable because they find a huge difference between actual and anticipated scenario, they would find this book a reassuring help.

This book intends to help all those selling people to sustain the pressures of selling, supervision, and targets. They would come to know that there is not much difference between them and the successful ones. The little difference they would find would be "that little extra effort at a right time".

There have been many theories which try to tell us about why a product sells or why not. Even after a hundred years in formal management education nobody has come anywhere near for a readymade, easy to consume capsule that would tell us about why a product sell. In the very typical, exclusive and diverse Indian scenario one is classically at the end of his wits and tries his own ways.

This book shall also try to emphasize on one simple fact, that most sales people have highly prejudiced ideas about fairness of life or vice versa. A.J. Cronin said that life is no straight and easy corridor where one can travel free and unhampered. He further said that life is a maze of alleys and passages and each such passage is separate lesson in learning.

Very sincerely put this book tries to decipher between the line's messages, which are most of the times missed either by design or default. All consultants, gurus, books, and even the teachers say that a marketing person needs to be smart, but rarely enough they talk about the key to smartness. This book would try to tell what is that one has to do to become smart. When you shall read this book, you would realise that you can relate with a lot of what it says. You may even find a solution to your chronic problems. It also intends to provide some fine tuning to people in advanced stages of sales careers.

Every salesperson has to somehow remember that whether successful or not his day would remain same. To be in the market every day, putting behind what happened yesterday, believing in the process and doing same things again and again is his lot. It is up to him whether he does it with a smile or a frown or even a grimace. Whatever else you learn or do under some unwanted influence is simply an illusion.

I would like to cite one simple example. All marketing people need to have a diary and maintain it. How many really do it? How many would like to, but cannot. In this book I have given in details about how a sales and marketing person should keep records. They would help the average sales person to become an outstanding variety.

At the end, if this book starts a process of self-evaluation in the minds of all those who matter and even if lives of a very few salespeople improve by a bit, I shall consider the purpose of the book is fulfilled.

***

INDEX

PART I

<u>YOU</u>

In any walk of life, in any activity of life if you want to be successful, remember YOU form the most important and vital ingredient. Everything minus "You" is virtually useless. The irony is that in most cases you do not know this simple fact. In exceptional cases maybe you know but the significance is apparently lost on "You".

I implore you to realise that unless *you wish* to be successful, this or for that matter any other book would be rendered useless. So, before you start reading this book in a casual way take a very serious and close look at you, both "outer you and "inner you".

<u>What do you think about yourself?</u>

Do you like what you see in the mirror? If yes you have a chance, if you do not like what you see in the mirror you are in a serious problem. Have you ever analysed as to why you do not like what you see? What part of you like and what you do not? I would ask you a simple question. Please answer as truthfully as you can.

Have you come across any other person who is like you? (Even in the cases of identical twins!) The answer should be a big NO.

Now stop for a second, take a deep breath, and start thinking about you. You have not seen any person like you because are an *exclusive edition* created by the God. If He so desired, he could have easily created millions like you, and you could have been one of the clones. But that is not the case. The reason is what you can do nobody else can. The point is to make you realise that you are in this world for some special reason and you are supposed to leave a lasting imprint on the canvas of the world. It may be anything and, in any field, but always remember that you are special.

Whatever is the reason which makes you think that can be a successful marketing/ sales person can be a great help to both of us. This is the primer which would help in creating a new You.

One of my bosses used to say that there are two types of people. One who can sell and the other who cannot. I partially agreed with him as I felt that there is third type of people who does not know they can sell.

The first category of the people is those who inadvertently follow the golden rules of selling, they do all the right things, follow all the "Do's" and without any apparent efforts are successful in sales. For such people this book might serve as a refresher course and they would be able to relate with many things said in the book.

The book is specifically for those who are shy, cannot sell (or think that they cannot sell) and most likely are in selling activity because they could not find anything else.

The "outer You"

You are tall or short, fair or dark, smart or simple, male or female, good and smart talker or not so smart talker, qualified or average, extrovert or introvert, so please be rest assured that you can be very successful in sales as a career. There are thousands if not millions in each of the category, who are very successful, so why not you?

Let us begin at the basics.

1. **Turnout -** As you are aware this is a military term and most of us have heard this when we were at the parade ground of NCC. Have you anytime thought why the NCO gave so much on the correct turnout? Let us begin at the top:

- Are you well groomed?
- Are you clean-shaved? Or with the routine stubble?
- Is your breath fresh?
- Do you smell good?
- Are you wearing a decent business shirt?
- Are your trousers matching to your shirt?
- Are you wearing a correct sized belt?
- Are you wearing a neatly polished pair of shoes? Preferably black and formal!
- Are your socks fresh?
- If you are required to wear a neck tie is it of the colour of the trouser?

Each of the above ten steps, is interlinked which would result in either a well-dressed person or a shabby person. Each step like the shoes, belt, adds to your get up. This sort of dress code increases your self-esteem and confidence. And of course, it adds dignity to your profile.

These days a lot of people are wearing spectacles. May be because of the TV or mobiles. Not many of us attach any importance to what sort of frame we select, we treat this aspect in a casual way. This is true with salesmen. Please check up. Do you realise that the spectacles are right up on your face, which is the most visible and creates the first impact on the people? *Wrong* spectacles on a *rightly dressed* up person can negate the impact. So, spend some time before you select the frame and the lenses.

So much talk about the dressing up brings out a natural question. Who is a well-dressed person? Luckily there is no thumb rule here, but there are many guidelines. The important thing is whether you are able to carry what you wear. There is an aspect of overdressing and low profile. We would understand this by following example.

Suppose, you are at a party, where you meet your friends, associates and clients. You had a good time and gone home. Next day in the morning there is usual talk about the party. A colleague asks you "Hey, do you remember Mrs. Sharma, and what she was wearing yesterday?" Now, if you remember she wearing a cream and black Banarasee saree, a contrast sleeveless blouse, a matching Bindi, a purse and all her ornaments, then the conclusion is simple. She was apparently overdressed. If she was more properly dressed then you might have said "She was looking great, wearing something rich and decent." The point here is that people should remember you as neatly and decently dressed person rather than your entire attire. Remember that you dress up to enhance your personality. People should never remember you as a *dressed-up doll* or a *dandy* person.

The basic purpose is to create a favourable first impression enabling a decent nonverbal communication.

Ladies, if you are reading my book, please forgive me for not dwelling on the topic of your clothes. I know my limits and so I do not dare to teach you anything. However, if you really want to learn then I suggest that seek guidance from any decently dressed lady you know and get some tips. As it is ladies have an inherent knack of knowing what suits them or not.

Remember, the best judge of your dress is inevitably you, yourself. As earlier said well-dressed is anything you wear which makes you feel confident. As a precaution, before you step out of your home, please spare a minute in front of a mirror. Ensure that everything is in place. Once you are sure of your dressing up, you can move out of the real purpose of actual action.

***

The Inner "You"

The inner "you" is the part which is extremely important in making or breaking you. The inner "you" is very personal as against the outer you. The outer you can be shaped or reshaped by instructions or practice more easily than the inner version. The inner you can be improved but it takes more time and even more serious teacher. There are many diverse inputs for the inner you and you must read some serious books on this topic. However, as far as the purpose of sales and marketing you should have following characters.

- Self-respect
- Confidence in the products you wish to sell
- Knowing exactly what you want
- A built-in process of continuous evaluation
- Sincerity and discipline
- Long term relation building rather than a short-term temporary gain.

There can be many more, but these would build you up and prepare you for a long-term success. Please understand that the process of sales is relatively simple. The repetitive nature makes it very taxing and affects the psyche of a person. Moreover, it has a component called a customer very unpredictable, erratic and many times just very taxing for the salesman. In any other activity of life, a person gets a workable experience in a couple of years, which helps him throughout his life. He can relax in the shadow of some specific intelligence. Not so in sales. Day after day, week after week, month after month and year after year he spends his time running after some improbable if not impossible targets. Whatever has been done in the last day, week, month or year is done with and it is of no relevance. Every day is fresh. Just imagine you doing same grind for thirty years and you would get the picture. Moreover, in a country like India, if you *sell* anything it is because of the quality of the products, reputation and the goodwill of the company, but when you do not perform it is only because you are incompetent. We would deal with each aspect in some detail.

1. **Self-respect:** The self-respect stems from thefact that you like yourself and you like what you do. You can very rarely feign self-esteem. There is no artificial self-respect. A person with correct self- respect can always be a good salesman, as he knows his own limits of bowing down. He also understands that selling is ideally an equal and fair exchange of goods and services. Self-respect can be ego or self-esteem. This is a highly volatile and readily perishable. One has to take special care to keep it alive and succeed in sales. Self-respect can be ego or self-esteem. This is a highly volatile and readily perishable. One has to take special care to keep it alive and succeed in sales.

2. **Confidence in products you sell:** when you join any company you are told that the products are world class. The prices and service are no issues. Very soon after a few encounters with the customers and competitors, the sheen starts wearing off.

Here a smart salesman should develop his own scale of ratings. Each product (in a multi products company) should be rated on a scale of one to ten. He can have his own parameters or he can take help from his supervisors. By doing this exercise he can have a correct product mix and can have a rational and correct approach to his product range. Remember customers prefer those salesmen who have a rational and reasonable approach than those who just say their products are the best.

1. **<u>Knowing exactly what you want:</u>** Apart from selling this applies to each aspect of your life. When you at least know what you want you stand on a sound footing. You have an idea of the probable outcome right in the beginning. It is suggested that you must carry weekly, monthly and yearly "what I want" cards with you. Your actions would be more balanced and more result oriented in your sales routines.

2. **<u>Inbuilt process of continuous evaluation:</u>** This is a real separator between the good, the better and the best salesmen. A mature salesperson must remember quite a few facts, such as his performance for the current month and the year. He must have meter like tendency towards the positives and the negatives around him. The events, the environment, the competition, and all such factors which may affect his routine. He must ask himself a question on a daily basis, which is "Am I where I should be?"

3. **<u>Sincerity and discipline:</u>** A person need to be sincere if he wants to be successful in anything he plans to do. More so in sales! If he has to meet someone, he has to follow the clock. If he has to be in a particular place he must be there. Irrespective of the response he gets from the market he has to maintain his routine. Please understand that the salesman can be rarely monitored by anybody except he himself. These days some companies have started the *minute to minute, place to place* monitoring by mobiles, which is one of the worst

things for the sales force and the organisation. The inner drive to excel is generated by the self-discipline. And the discipline starts TODAY, so never plan it for tomorrow.

4. **<u>Long term relationship building approach than temporary gains:</u>** If youare sincere, disciplined and have something better to offer you can be assured of success. More often than not the trust created by the salesperson results in orders than the typically promoted factors like price, quality and others.

Each customer should be made to feel like a very special and valuable person. The approach from a salesman should be more to solve the problems and clearing the bottlenecks rather than merely pushing for products. Continuous providing of good services, advice, suggestions would always generate repeat orders. And repeat orders is the basic aim of the marketing and sales. The thumb rule is that one satisfied customer is equal to five new one-time buyers. The efforts are less the trust is more.

***

PART II
EVERYONE IS A SALESMAN!
ARE YOU?
Conventional marketing is a very big and complex activity and most of the common people find it beyond their comprehension. People have some notions, but the all-important clarity is lacking. We hear people talking about marketing as a process, which someone else is supposed to do and they underline that they are not the part of the same. Some people specifically disassociate with marketing, proudly saying that it is not their cup of tea. The declare that they cannot sell. This statement is very amazing and let us analyse why.

Do you realise that you are a part of a very intelligent species which thrives in a society, and has successfully survived the demands of the very unforgiving master which is referred to as The Nature? Humans have been the least endowed as far as the physical attributes are concerned. Lions and tigers have strength, stealth and grace. Elephants have physical might, birds can fly, vipers have venom, panthers can run fastest while horses can run very incredible long distances, the list goes on and on. But none of these, rules the world! Who rules? You, my friend you! And why? Because you have a brain the seat of intelligence which has found effective ways to overcome the physical minuses. Very pleasing statement! And how much of this organ is used by a common man? In spite of the evolution spread across millions of years you would be surprised that the brain of the great Einstein is preserved, stored and researched. He used just two percent more than what we are supposed to. We use less than five percent of the available potential of the brain in the entire life time.

You would be wondering. Why this build up? The reason is simple. I want to remind you that before you say that you cannot do a thing, please ask yourself a question. Do you have any unused capacity of your brain? Suddenly you would realise that nothing is impossible. May be a bit improbable, but never impossible, when you set your mind on, pursue and persevere with. If you really wish, want something you would do anything and accomplish anything.

I am trying to invite your attention to a basic fact that you and you alone are the most "magical component" of anything you undertake. You may have the best situations, people, equipment, plenty of funds, and yet without you and your involvement you have best chance of failing.

Please think. If you are so important so vital, why you have been so casual, so underrated, to such an extent that you almost cease to exist?

Let us come back to the point whether you can sell or not? I believe that every person is a born salesman. Every man is selling something throughout his life. Either he is selling to someone or some one is selling to him. This is a lifelong process, but the funny part is that this comes to us in natural way but not in a professional way. We just do not accept that we can sell.

Right from childhood we use the selling techniques. We promote ourselves for a role in a musical, or a drama, for a class monitorship or many such activities. We are doing everything that a salesman does, but we are not aware. We check for the moods of our parents (before we put forth the demand for a motorcycle), we check up the financial environment of our household, we go out of our normal ways and are on our best behaviour, before we actually initiate our sale. You would agree that we rarely failed. In the language of sales, you closed the deal formally. The kids and salesmen have one thing in common trait. They do not take **no** for an answer.

Once the formal education is over and done with the hardest phase in the life of a young man starts. He prepares his biodata, and sends it to the future employers. Biodata is the best **sales pitch,** he has undertaken. He promotes himself, **by** projecting his qualities, skills and experience. In sales it is called detailing.

He or she definitely sell him or her for a job, promotion, or for a foreign assignment. Don't you do this?

Are you not a born salesman?

But in the course of your career, when you feel that you are settled, you suddenly find that you have lost the knack of selling. And you start to proclaim that you cannot sell. It is funny! The skill which you have so far so successfully used is suddenly gone. You may be educated in any discipline, such as science, commerce, engineering, medicine, law, or fine arts Please rest assured that to reach the top bracket you would have to use your inherent skills of salesmanship. Watch all the top people in any profession they would have the following qualities, either in part or full.

- They dress well
- They know their subject well
- They have a knack of communication
- They have a high level of pleasant persuasion
- They generally do not take no for an answer
- They have a sense of timing
- They are very aware of the changes in environment around them
- They give very good services to their clients.

Now if you notice that the above are the things which a salesman has to do throughout his life. But if you ask any of the above whether he can sell and the answer would be a bug No.

Why this happens? I have tried to rationalise the instant aversion to sales. The selling probably reminds them of the discomfort they had to face in the initial stages of their careers, they want to get away with it. Now they are quite **settled, successful and nothing to do with the below level selling.**

What is the origin of this feeling of discomfort?

1. In the past you were imposing at least you felt so, for

your own products or services, now there is no such need.

2. Fear of rejection. In the early stage of your careers, you were rejected many times, but you somehow sustained. There was no ego prestige or social status attached so it did not matter. You knew that the rejection was not personal. It was painful but it was a part of life. To understand that the rejection is more idea oriented takes some time. The pain that comes with rejection is very personal.

3. Fear of failure. When you put the idea, concept or a product you supplement it with your personality, ego and pride so when it fails, it hurts. Does it mean that the fear of failures is only with the beginners? No, it is not so. In fact, the stakes are much more and bigger for the successful people. Sunil Gavaskar, the original little master said that in spite of hundreds by the dozens, after so much success every time he went to open the innings he had the same number of butter flies in his stomach as he had when he made the debut. The anxiety was even more prominent. If this is true then how come the successful people appear so serene, so calm on the outside? Inside they are as afraid as the common beginner, but they have somehow learnt to have a better cover up on their doubts. They have understood that it is a matter of time before the fear fades away. Please understand if are afraid to fail you may never even start in the first place. The importance of failures is to be understood. It is only on the dark backdrop of failures the success shines. Success in isolation, that is, without failure has no meaning. The scale of success is measured on the volume of failures. The humility to accept failures can be the first step of the success, successful people

even if they know that they would fail never reduce the levels of efforts. The successful people have learnt the trick of using their past failures as a spring board rather than a hammock. They do not recline and regret. Practice in a perfect way if you want to become perfect or you would be perfect in wrong things. Whatever makes you uncomfortable, **do it until you are a master of the same.** If you are afraid, or conscious of talking to strangers, then just talk to more strangers. It would make a perfect person for a cold call in the future.

4. Fear of a change. When a person is in his thirties, he is more often than not fallen in to a groove. The set routine of life makes him very comfortable. He has adjusted to the limits of earnings and limits of success. He has accepted his lots as his destiny and is at least outwardly happy. He anticipates that because he has so far survived, he would continue to do so. As a matter of fact, he starts calling his life as a **life style. He tries to justify, protect, and defend** his present status and says that it is the best he could have bargained for. But deep down in his mind he knows that he could have been better. Further he knows that he alone is responsible for his present lots, but he rarely acknowledges the fact. He blames his parents, teachers, family but never blames himself. He is in a dark cave and he is in a frustrated state of mind. Everyone knows that if you have to change the way you live you have to change the way you think. Some do change the ways they think and then they change their lots. Steve Jobs is a classic example. He succeeded twice on a scale which is incomprehensible to most of us.

Finally, what creates panic in the minds who say that they cannot sell, who say that selling is not their cup of tea is the basic fact that unlike other professions there is no place to hide in the sales. You are afraid of the periodical appraisals, reviews where in your performance is ruthlessly analysed. The weekly, monthly, quarterly and annual appraisals can be very painful and exhausting.

But with all these aspects sales can be a very interesting activity and career. It gives you an accelerated exposure and you are generally smarter than the rest of the world. Moreover, if you really think so can you be really away from the sales? Probably no!

So, when you next time say that cannot sell…. take a pause, think for a moment and then only say whatever comes to your mind.

***

PART III

<u>THE MARKET</u>

The market is the actual field where all your inherent and acquired skills as a marketer and or salesman are duly tested on a day-to-day basis. It can turn out be a battlefield or a walk in a garden depending upon many things. Till today no exact definition of market is actually available, but it is a place that is responsible for commercial transactions beyond any reasonable limits. It encompasses and controls a really huge activity which is throughout the world across the countries, time zones, races, religions, caste, creed and currencies. Over a period of centuries, it has evolved in to a mind-boggling proportion, speed, and volumes. So many different products, so many classes of services, so many industries, so many different salesmen, and so many different customers are daily involved in the *making* or sometimes *breaking* of a viable market.

As a salesman you should know that different products need different expertise and approaches. On the whole, the market can be classified into following:

1. Consumer
2. Consumables
3. Consumer durables
4. Institutional
5. Industrial
6. Trade
7. Cooperative
8. Corporate.
9. Conceptual
10. Space marketing
11. Ethical or pharma sales
12. Government sales
13. Shopping malls.
14. Digital and On-line marketing

May be in the future some more categories would be added but the basic rules would generally be same as they are today. I have tried to analyse the basic needs for dealing in each of the types in this chapter. Once you learn the basic selling you would need to learn specific tricks of the trade. A little bit of fine tuning is needed on a continuous basis, to maximise the benefits as different products would need different approaches.

1. **Consumer:** Consumer market where we get involved on a daily basis as a consumer or as a salesman and of course the shop owners. The category of the product has very little to do on product-to-product basis. This is a fine example of many consumers reaching one place for

many products. The individual stakes are comparatively less (as the cost of product is less), but the cumulative impacts can be huge. Does it mean that this particular segment is easy to handle and can be managed with relative ease? No, not at all! The actual time of interaction of the consumer and the salesman is minimal. No sales pitches. The dealer plays an important role. The point of purchase can be important at as on today. This segment is facing serious challenges from the supermarkets, online sales etc. but so far it has survived in a decent manner. Philip Kotler in one of his predictions had said that the display space and ease of foot fall would decide the survival of retail sales activity. He was right as usual. There is a fierce fight for the space in the shops. The product displays are at premiums. The points of purchase (POP) promotional activities are very cutthroat and strenuous. Earlier the shopkeepers were less demanding, now they have also picked the tricks of the trade. So, they demand their pound of flesh in the trade promotions. All major players like Colgate, Godrej, P&G, HLL, Nirma, Patanjali, Dabur, Nestle, Cadbury, Novino batteries, oils, cosmetics, fight literally for an inch of the display space. In fact, the daily sales reports have a designated section on the display of each outlet. Company like Hindustan Lever has one of the most detailed and comprehensive reports. How much data is generated and how much it is put to improve the lots of the consumer is a point of debate and serious research.

However, the salesman who manages the consumer product ranges should have preferably following profile.

- He should be a fast worker as he has to contact 100 counters per day.
- He should evoke trust and should be well behaved. Mild person is more likely to succeed.
- He may not be very intelligent but must have some basic integrity. He needs a honeybee approach.
- Most of the retailers would tell you that they prefer to see same person representing same company for some length of time. The major complaint is that the salesmen change too soon for their comfort. The lack of trust emerges as the result.

One has to really feel for the persons in consumer sales and appreciate their unending and many times unforgiving grind. It is not at all easy to contact hundred counters on a daily basis for years to come. They do this monotonous routine for almost thirty years, before burning out. The irony is that even after such a vicious grind they rarely know anything very little about actual selling much less about marketing. Even today with all digital warfare the salesman still remains the final link of the entire marketing strategy designed by either a designated brand manager and /or marketing manager. Even today the line sales people are yet to receive the credit due to them. With the mobile tabs and scrutiny, the only human participant is reduced to a mechanical input.

It is of common knowledge that the 4 Bs are the most difficult product ranges to handle. They are Bulbs/ Batteries/ Biscuits and Blades. These are the fastest changing fields and to keep up to the ever-changing requirements of these B's turn out the toughest and the best salesmen in the consumer field.

2. **<u>Consumables</u>**- This category is more or less similar to the earlier consumer except that in here the *same* customers are have to be serviced more often. The same can be also attached to the industrial marketing. It is more dependent on dealers than the consumer.

3. **<u>Consumer Durables</u>**- This category is the so-called glamourous range of products. Televisions, refrigerators, washing machines, air conditioners, coolers, vacuum cleaners, food processors/ mixers, mobiles, together form a "White Goods Category". The atmosphere is very plush, posh, very well-lit and almost jazzy type. Today again this sector is facing the crisis due to digital marketing like Amazon, and others. The dealer here also deals with retails but the difference is in the frequency of buying. The consumer durables are purchased mostly once in a lifetime. If very optimistically put it may be once in ten years. Then what makes this sector tick? The margins used to be very good till in the late eighties of last century. Some companies enjoyed advance bookings, shortages, and even premiums. But it was too good to last. In the beginning of the nineties the slump had started. The tactics changed. The giants like Sony, LG, started their own showrooms. There was a huge boom in the supermarkets. Like Big Bazar, Reliance, and so many others. The retail outlet dealer was suffering very badly. Later the super bazars were put to dust by the online marketing companies like Amazon, Snapdeal. The outlets were reduced by more than half. They either closed or diversified. The only lever or advantages the lonely dealer had been the advantage of providing credit to the customers.

Earlier and the first to enter with the hire purchase schemes was unexpectedly the Citi Bank. It was the reason for the change in the demand equation. Just a few months later State Bank of India followed with a Big Buy scheme. Now every finance company worth its name has a plan or two for all those who want to buy but have no ready cash. The advertisements of *zero percent interest* or "Just pay 100 and take home a TV/Washing Machine/ even a car." Type ads are abundant in the trade. This is one of the major reasons because of which this consumer durable trade is flourishing. It is surprising to see the manufacturers like Bajaj have their own finance company. It is a miracle of the last decade. The banks and the finance companies promote their schemes with such a heavy hand that most gullible customers feel that they are getting the product almost as a gift. Sadly, this is too big a game with even bigger rackets. The salesman in this category has to be sincere towards the company he works for or else his days are numbered. He has to be smart, clear headed, and pretty fair towards the products, dealers and the customers. If this equilibrium is not achieved, it would result in a threat to his existence. The dealers are more powerful, they have a hotline to the top brass of the company and hence they can overpower the salesperson with ease. Considering all odds, it can be safely said that the duty of the salesman in the white goods category is to **convert the pull** created by heavy advertisements in to **actual conversion** in to revenue at the retail counter. if he fails the entire campaign and promo schemes would be utterly wasted.

The salesman in this area have evolved into extra smooth variety which is quite irritating most of the times. But that is how it is.

4) **<u>Institutional</u>**: Institutional sales can be termed as an off shoot of the hire and purchase schemes. The basic advantage is bulk purchase at a single point. Moreover, you have already taken care of the competition. You have as clear a field as you can ever wish to have. This is a very specialised job and needs various skills like, sustained relationship building, extra attention to services offered and continuous follow up. You have to be aware that your competitors are also on the prowl to spoil your party. The span of time from the initiation of the enquiry to the actual placement of the order and further smooth execution may be six months or even more. So before starting the process the salesman must check that the person, the decision maker would be around for at least one year. There are so many examples where a near complete deal fall apart because of the transfers or even the retirements of the dealing authority. The absolute pain of reporting the deal going bust. All the efforts of earlier six months, and high sales projections fall flat and your management would be mad at you. The ridicule is too heavy. The second thing to be primarily checked is the financial condition of the prospect. If it is a government department or undertaking then the policy must remain at least for one year. The third and probably the most important thing is how closely you can handle the deal. Or else you would do all the hard work, toil for months and end up in getting nothing. Some smarter competitor would jump in with lesser prices and just snatch the deal. The only things that change in the order is the name of the product and the lower price. The officers have a readymade offer with proper justification and even approvals. The fewer persons know about your deal is the only security you have. The other people from the department also have their axes to grind. They also

have their contacts. And never forget you own colleagues they can backstab at the first chance. So, be very careful and then you may be really enjoying the fruits of success.

5. **Industrial**: The industrial sector is the hardest or the easiest selling area depending upon what types of industries you are supposed to contact. Let us see the harder part first.

The customer here is sharp. Most likely he is more intelligent and more experienced. He is more qualified and he may be an expert in the field say manufacturing or maintenance. He sees no point in dealing with incompetent salesman. He is already overstressed. And hence he may have very little tolerance levels. Actually, there is no reason for anyone to tolerate a salesman's stupidity. Trying to *convince* such a tough professional is a waste of time. If you try the age-old approach of "Our product is the best, cheapest, etc.... etc" you have lost the match without a ball being bowled. Here he is doing what he knows best for the last ten years and suddenly a most unlikely person in the form of the salesman trying to tell him that he would do better if he follows the salesman.

To deal with these you have to be thorough, in your product knowledge, technology used, and its practical and actual application in the process used by them. In industry what sells is the correct demo of the product than the sales pitch. What he sees he does either agree or does not. Talking has to be replaced by doing.

One more difficult part in the industrial sales is the limited number of customers. You have to establish yourself first then your products. Moreover, these days the industries barring a few are in a mess, they are what is known as hand to mouth. Hence the salesman has to be very clear about the credit terms, delivery schedules and payment terms.

After all the difficulties, the *easy part* comes from the fact that they know exactly what they want. Product wise and pricewise it is a race between you and the competition. One more easy thing is what was the hard part initially. You must recall the time you had to spend to make the industrial customer for shifting from his conventional to your type of products. So, you can be assured that unless your product quality dips you have a steady flow of orders. Salesman has to know the concept of down time in the industry and should take care that his products or their shortage is not the reason for the downtime. When you have an established channel, it becomes easy for you introduce new ranges and improved versions of existing products. Industrial selling is a difficult, demanding exercise but it is also gratifying because it deals in huge numbers and revenue.

<u>6.Trade:</u> The trade market is all inclusive term and probably teaches maximum to the aspiring sales and marketing professional. Trade market is mainly a combination of stockists, dealers, sales partners, and all such facilities which are

Included in the activity called trade. The trading term has different meaning when referred to in the context of the shares and stock market.

TRADE MARKET

Trade

Dealers is a special category and part of the society. The role of dealer gets defined and reviewed in every society depending upon the lifestyle of the particular society. The complicated relationship between the dealer and the producer of the goods is very difficult to understand and operate. There is trust or lack of it, there is a feeling of association or a fight for the share of the profit, the see saw is very interesting. The salesman who understands the dealers and their role in the overall development of the company generally finds a balance and leads a comfortable life. If trade business is properly handled it can be very beneficial for the manufacturer. The criteria on which the dealership is finalised can be the key to the later success. It should be rational and process based rather than based on caste, community, region, religion or even language.

These days some new terms are used. They are as follows.

SPA- Sales Promotion Agents

DCA- Dealer cum Applicator

Partners in Trade

Some more would be coming as the pattern of the sales and distribution would change. Again, Indians have shown an unnecessary hurry in adopting the American pattern over their traditional ways which helped them to rule the world for thousands of years.

Coming back to our salesman. He must remember one primary thing to avoid future complications. "That he is *paid by the company* he works for and that the company would keep doing so long as the dealers perform as per the norms of the company. The thin line always exists between the manufacturer and the dealers which must be maintained. It is comparable to the relationship in the family like the real brothers and cousins. The trade market actually teaches the salesman much more than he could ever learn by way of training in the company. Each dealer is a different, separate pulsating *entity* and presents exclusive and customised set of advantages and problems. Hence each is special!

7. Co-operative sector: This sector is a relatively new wing of sales activity. It started somewhere in early sixties. It is very peculiar to the Indian politics and the political leadership *generally rules and exploits* this sector. It is one of the darkest examples of power misuse and personal agenda. However, gladly there are happy exceptions in Amul, Lijjat.

Coming back to our salesman! He would be dealing with cooperative businesses if he is selling seeds, fertilisers, pump sets, irrigation systems, pesticides, or the school accessories as well as the items dealt by the social welfare ministry. The purchases are in huge quantities and hence a lot is at stake. Generally, the purchase is made by the society which can be either consumer society or consumer credit society. The society can be the primary model for the trade in rural market. If your products are of the rural type, you must learn all aspects of cooperative trade. The president, the secretary and in some cases the technical officer form the decision-making unit. With the advent of easy finance schemes this channel enjoys the exclusive attention and can be very effective if properly used.

8. Corporate: When the marketing is done at the corporate management level it can be called as the corporate marketing. One example may explain.

The story goes like this: A very big multinational organization having its corporate office in Mumbai, was negotiating an extraordinary deal in Bangalore. It was in crores of rupees. The direct demand officer, (DDO) was of the level of a Deputy Chief Engineer in the concerned government department. The order was delayed and was almost lost because the Bangalore office of the company could not generate enough force. Incidentally, the Chairman of the company was in Bangalore. He was being briefed by the concerned regional manager. The on-the-spot feedback on the status of the almost lost order, was too much for the firebrand new generation Chairman. He could not accept and hence visited the office of the DCE. He went unannounced. The Chairman sent his visiting card. The DCE was out of his wits and came running out of his office, greeted the Chairman, and was waiting for any clue for the visit. The DCE was very aware that the Chairman was held in very high esteem by the department bosses, including the Minister. The Chairman was a smart person. He talked about everything except his own company. When enough steam was created to cook everything up, the Chairman got up to leave and wished the best to the DCE. And just when he was leaving, he as a parting remark he informed the DCE that his Bangalore office was talking about some order that was held up. Further he said that if there was anything he could do for the same.

Can you guess what happened afterwards? Next week the order was received by at Bangalore Regional Office. This time around the regional manager was out of his wits, because he never knew that the Chairman had visited the DCE out of turn. His suspense ended when the marketing manager told him the story during their monthly meeting at Mumbai.

Please note that such a thing happens once in a decade.

9.Conceptual- One more term that is the gift of the late nineties which earned quite a reputation is the conceptual selling/ marketing. After the so-called opening of the market in the futuristic conditions there was either a great influx of foreign ideas, concepts and product lines. There was appointed reference to anything that was Indian and it was promoted that whatever was western was better. After the outbreak of many endemics and pandemics the bubble has finally burst. But in those days, it was very fashionable to call the products as conceptual etc. The concepts like cosmetics, wellness products, linen, cotton, minimum access surgeries, epoxy materials, high quality non-stick coatings, vacuum cleaners, smps, ultra sound and MRI imaging are some of the few one can recall. Some were really very stunning while others were not so. But these ranges created a sales force which was very similar to the missionaries. They were talking of things ahead of the present time to the people who were pretty rigid. The secret of the success was in the skill with which you dispersed the new knowledge without ever creating a single bit of antagonism. The basic thing was *not to say* anything negative about the present and conventional methods or equipment. The salesman had to acknowledge right in the beginning about the services so far given by the traditional methods. This simple approach made the customer to feel smart and good about himself. NOW, if the customer has to continue being smart and further updated then should just listen to what the salesman had to say. He would adopt the new products because he wants to. That too for the betterment of his own activity and earn more revenue and respect.

The concept marketers were helped beyond any reasonable limits by the people who were in the top tier of the society. The concept of utility, and economy was slowly replaced by in step with the western world. And supposedly equal to them. The concept marketers almost always concentrated on the younger generations.

<u>10. Space Marketing</u>- When a person is comfortable with twenty-four hours deadlines or even less, he should think of going in the field of space marketing. In common language it means collecting advertisements for the daily newspapers, magazines and other print media. Please note it is one of the most interesting and toughest fields to work in. You are tested on a daily basis that too on a straight forward centimetre by centimetre. The competition activity is also very visible. In fact, the daily meeting of the press can be very pleasant or very explosive. The customer is given a brief based on the readership, ad recall, cost per view and many such things. It is very flashy and unpredictable market. The figures are generally cooked up, if not manipulated.

a) Print Media: In space marketing the basic tools are the ABC (Audit Bureau of Circulation) NRS (National Readership Survey) and a few others. The agencies involved are National Readership Survey Council, INS (Indian News Society), AAAI (Advertising Associations of India) and the ABC. Despite of the big names the data still needs to be discounted and evaluated by different standards. Again, the relationship between the circulation and the readership has never been analysed in a way it should be. Maybe, it is because the publications are run by the politicians who are rarely interested in the truth. As a media manager one has to learn the relationship of the newsprint consumption, and the actual figure of circulation. We are very smart and have an ability to exploit any possible loopholes in any system. What baffles any sensible person is the incorrect circulation figures?

One of my media manager friends told me that the discount factor is about thirty percent less than the reported figures. Secondly the analysis of demography of the readership is very peculiar to say the least. The sample size of the survey is very rarely reported correctly. So even after the data, its analysis, and smooth language of the space selling person the media managers depend upon the age-old system. So, the smart marketing people who design the media campaigns generally go by the response to the *actual response coupons and /or mail box responses rather* than the circulation, readership, and ABC analysis.

As reader of any newspaper, you can find by your own interest in any advertisements you see daily. The time spent on reading the newspaper is generally in minutes. Project your figures and you would have a fair idea about the efficacy of the advertisements. Economic Times generally carries the updated versions of the NRS as well as the TRP figures. They help as a light house.

When every newspaper or publication claims number one in one or the other category. To test these claims is very essential for the correct efficacy of the media management. Media test marketing is a must or your money just would evaporate very fast.

But as earlier said space marketing is a very challenging field. In all other fields the deadline is on a monthly basis. In print media it is twenty-four hours. What is printed today has no relevance tomorrow. Very few in sales can cope with this relentless pressure of performing. Add to this a boss who knows what he should know and then you may not have a single day of happiness. But if you are working for a decent publication and performing well as per the expectations of your boss space marketing is the best field to work in.

b) Audio Visual media: What can one really say about this very jazzy, fast, ruthless, and flashy field? When people say AV media as the ultimate monster created in the 20th century I tend to agree. The lack of quality, the coarse clothes or lack of them, the mindless promotion of mediocrity, the frequency of advertisements, is really beyond any comprehensions. They have TRP very similar to the ABC etc.

What business are they really in? They are in the business of revenue generation, nothing else. Rest whatever they do, is the classical moh maya as in the Hindu philosophy. They make us watch the advertisements whether we want to or not. In the earlier days of television and NET we could at least switch the channels off or start surfing for the channels. They are smart and they have now <u>synchronised</u> the advertisements so even if you search for other channels you end up watching something you never want to buy. Their ill effect on the sub conscious minds is visible. I am really worried for the next generations. They must have a heart of steel to escape from the effects of monstrous hammering of the advertisement's day in and day out. Once in a while you may see a good commercial but that is an exception. The relationship between the concept of the ad and the products is microscopic to say the least. Many times, you remember the ads but not the product and vice versa. What we see on the screen is quite disgusting but what we hear about the backstage activities of the ad agencies, models, their life styles are devastating. Why we have to see the ads of condom, sanitary napkins, energy capsules, on the family shows? Are they I really needed? We are moving away from the ethos, traditions, culture of our great nation and sadly no body is bothered. I feel that the Indians are masters in giving up things. No other country, no other community has given up so much of their own culture and adopted trash from outside. You can list at least thousand things which we have left.

But again, who are we to change what is happening? The AV field is a specialised field. The person here has to be a visionary to predict the future of any ad campaign. Whatever little I have seen of this huge industry makes me shudder. Only thing I can say this field requires a particular type to succeed if you are a little loud, extra smooth, very good in languages, very flexible about working hours, late nights, party animal, then and then only you should think of entering this razzle dazzle of a field. What we are talking is only for the marketing aspect.

11. Ethical (Pharmaceutical)markets: One of the most glamourised markets in the last century is now on the verge of losing all its sheen. The ethical part is diminishing very fast. The cuts, the commissions, the tax evasions, the foreign trips, the unnecessary prescriptions, are some of the things which can be reviewed.

Earlier it used to be a huge market which used to cater hundreds of millions of people on a daily basis. The people who worked here were smartly dressed, and had earned a respect from the field. In fact, in the early seventies any person wearing a neck tie was automatically associated with pharma sales. The term was M.R. As a student of sales and marketing I am always fascinated by these people and their activity. Also, I have healthy respect for these types. If we have to use the current term *of bio bubble* then these people have their own variety of different if not distinguished business bubble. The ethical detailing as they call it is easy and difficult. They deal with one of the most hyped and qualified community of the society *the doctors*. To talk to, to motivate the doctor to prescribe the medicines manufactured by your company is no mean feat. Everyone in India knows about the majority of the problems in the medical and pharma field. Many of my friends are working in pharma field have narrated experiences about the "noble" profession. In the recent extra ordinary pandemic situation stories from medical field were shocking and fascinating. We are not discussing the *what should be done aspect* so I would come back to pharma selling. No profession is independent of the society and medicine sadly is no exception.

The MR as he is called is now a term just like a manager. There is no gender bias. Many ladies have chosen pharma selling as their career and they are performing admirably.

Ladies probably have an inherent talent for counselling and convincing and that is very visible in the activity. Very surprisingly, even if the MR is one of the most visible persons, he rarely sees his actual customer. The process of pharma selling is very typical. A company manufactures or formulates as it is referred to some medicines, its designated MR details the products to the doctors, then doctor prescribes some of the products to the patients and some retailers then actually sell these products to the consumers. So simple, is it? And throughout the process the MR is responsible for the effective movement of the products. It is one of the most coordinated processes as each component rarely sees the other and depends fully on his participation.

How difficult it must be to estimate the demand of a particular drug, then to ensure the proper detailing to the prescribing doctors, then ensuring that the appropriate area retailers maintain the required stocks for the selling. The entire process is simply astonishing and that it continues is almost a miracle, as there is no contact with the actual consumer at the cash conversion point of purchase. For the companies with some reputation like Glaxo, Cipla, Abbot, Torrent, Cadilla, and many others it may be relatively easy. But can you spare a thought for a MR of say a company called "Ganga Mata Pharma". What must be his pitch, how he must be creatin demand, and later fulfil it? It is simply amazing!

These days many negative aspects are attached to pharma selling but they are not as rule. So even today the old routine of pharma selling is followed.

Yes, the pharma companies used to have the best training facilities in our country. The results were bearing it out. Companies like Ciba, Pfizer had a long induction and then on the job training programs. There was a visible difference in a person. He came out almost as a new version. Now in spite of the glow and shine or the money involved the pharma sales people are under tremendous pressure and generally look tense. The relaxed approach is gone. The pressure of targets is very visible. What ails this once very promising industry is very complex and needs a detailed review and analysis. Is it because medical profession is a pale shadow of it earlier noble version? Or is it because the unethical promotion? Or is it because the mediocrity of the doctors or the MRs? Is it the combination of pharma and insurance which is killing the nobility?

The sales person in other fields must take heart from these pharma sales people and do their jobs with more interest and determination for the simple and one reason that they can at least see their customers.

12.The Government: It is one of the largest buyers of anything under the blue. It is a wonderland like field and those like Alice have only a free access to the same. This market is generally not open for lesser mortals like us. There are authorised and unauthorised agents. Sadly, the second version is more prominent even today. Most of the funds were and are spent over those products which the government may never need. Why? Because some nephew or son in law of some minister may have the agency for this range of products. Millions of rupees are still wasted. May be this is the area which is the road to the sudden affluence of some politically connected people in India. You may recall hundred stories of rags to riches stories in your area. Multiply them for each such area and you may have the idea about the extent of the loot and corruption. Again, this is not the scope of this essay. But sales can never be discussed in isolation.

There are many reasons and many processes which are used, manipulated and twisted to suit the requirement of pleasing the ministers. The employees are bound by the rules and precedents. They are experts in reducing the pace and efficiency of the process. Everything on paper is done correctly, following all rules laid down by the people probably living in the caves. The people even from Mughal era would have found the rules of government *out of date*.

But in spite of all these *stringent* rules there are many examples of matchboxes sold for hundred rupees each, a pen for twenty rupees, when these things are available for one rupee per piece. Why this happens? Because nobody from top to bottom is interested in anything except his own percentage from the deal. Tremendous intentional inertia, corruption, favouritism, nepotism, under hand dealings are the major features of this huge irresponsibly handled sector. The irony further is that all people here are qualified and technically competent, but they lack simple integrity. The quality control in government sector is a big joke. Whether it is simple mid-day meals for the deprived or *the software* for the income tax department of central government. The cases of corruptions are never solved because the judiciary is also of questionable integrity.

<u>Just one example:</u>

In the recent past a state electricity board has levied a new levy on the hapless consumers. It is called transmission losses. This is a case of utter shamelessness. Let us see why?

The state electricity boards called as SEBs have the one of the largest pools of technical competence in form of the engineers. Some body technically qualified in the SEB specified the sizes of the conductors, or transmission lines. They were of course within the acceptable tolerance levels. Somebody more experienced than the middle level engineer must have approved the specifications and the cost. Some body very senior in the materials then procured the lines. So far so good. No auditor can do anything.

Now suddenly the transmission lines have started to incur more transmission losses. Why?

Who bears the brunt? Of course, the consumer! What happens to all those qualified technically competent people? Nothing! They are enjoying the commissions! The consumer suffers because the states have monopoly. That is one more very peculiar aspect. How all monopoly sectors in government like public transport, railways, steel, cement, power, aluminium, and even gold are making huge losses? It is really comical that people like HP, IOL, SAIL, CIL need a fleet of marketing staff. They may at the most the distribution managers but marketing: a big joke!

Any way, if a salesman chooses to sell in government department, he must have following skills.

- He must be very good in percentages.
- He must develop a thick skin
- No inklings about quality, and about misuse of public money.
- A benign attitude towards corruption
- Additionally, hc must have expertise in wines and liquors.

Any person who has dealt with government selling would tell you the government somehow works is a miracle. One expert said that after he had a stint in government sales he started believing in God.

He should also have a clear idea about all purchase procedures, like DGS&D, CSPO, CSD, RATE Contracts, tenders and their types, digital tendering, digital signatures, and all topical new things that enter the department. One small bit of relevant information is worth in millions of rupees. He should be aware of 3 quotations, 5/3/2 percentages, and its distribution, measurement book (MB) and every small trick of this amazing trade.

***

13. The shopping malls/ super markets: The shopping malls were introduced to Indians in the last decade of last century. The top of the recall is the Big Bazar, or Reliance Super Fresh, and many such who had a great time and now are not seen. Estimated by the Statista.com the estimated number in India is a staggering 12.8 million which includes the traditional variety. The number of customers in the segment is so huge that the top brands in the world are drooling over the prospects of the entry in this segment. There are many socio economic, and demographic issues which would be emerging from this type of markets. Classically the markets developed in the following sequence. A salesman went to customers, then customer started visiting a shop, then many shops in the same area formed the markets, development of wholesale and retails, home delivery types, and even today the interchange is going on. The supermarkets tried to combine many of these features in the projects.

However, the concept of supermarkets is still not very popular in Indian markets. They have become a success in the metro and the minimetro cities. But the traditional market is still surviving is a good thing. The initial benefits offered by the supermarkets are temporary and then the fleecing of the customers starts. Moreover, Indian consumer laws are lax and they do not offer any worthwhile protection to the consumer. The goods return policy, the quality checks, the ambiance, do not match with the international regulations and if they do the implementation is pathetic.

The younger generation is more likely to adopt the culture of supermarkets and malls. The concept of spending a day at the mall is more appealing to them. Buying, eating outside, entertainment by way multiplexes, and even dining at the same place is alluring only to them. The plush atmosphere actually repels the traditional customers. They are wise to know that ultimately every comfort comes out of their pockets.

Coming back to sales aspect one has to concede that these mega stores have changed the concepts of buying. So, almost companies have separate sales force and policies which cater to the megastores. The rates are different, very low as compared to normal wholesalers. The selling in bulk is a special skill and the salesman who have it can be very happy selling to the malls. Again, the supplier has a very little say in the management or display of goods. Everything is chargeable, each inch of the space is severely fought for. The competition is very cutthroat. The quantities are mindboggling, but it is a twenty-four-seven job. If the entry of companies like Costco, Walmart, is seen in the near future then the market of the traditional retail is in deep trouble. The small trader can never compete with these company setups. The old law of big fish eats small fish is very much applicable. The customer has to find what suits him.

For a salesperson this can be like the institutional sales.

14 Digital/ Online/ Web markets: The latest to enter the madness called selling is the digital market. The models developed by Amazon, Snapdeal, Alibaba, has simply zapped the world. No wonder that amazon is in the top three of the world ranking. It is a beautiful concept which does not need any traditional set up. They do not need shops, malls, godowns, and even then, they have captured a major share of the global market. They have no limits for products, production schedules, no labour unions, no area restriction, no language bars, no maps and hence a simple product can reach the globe. The phenomenal success is due to the great vision of the founders.

Coming back to sales aspect, a significant change is there. The change is in the contact mechanism. The entire aspect of *attention* in the classical AIDA model is taken care of by the company software people. The sales people are involved in the vendor development rather than the customer development. This activity is still running on only a few of its million legs. It has already sent ripples in the traditional markets.

Salesman in this area has to be very close to the ground, very able to communicate at least in India with very suspicious small-time artisans, and sometimes cottage industry. In the recent past even the automobile market has shifted to the online version. The key words here are B2B, niche, auction market places, crowdfunding, pocket friendly, MVP, SaaS, and many more. This is a very fast and happening market and things change in an instant. The salesman has to be tech savvy, friendly and a trouble shooter type.

I think we have covered almost all categories of markets, however they keep on merging or separating depending upon place, population, products, prices and other famous Ps of marketing.

***

Part IV
<u>You and Market</u>

By now we have seen what you are and what are the likely places called the market are. They are also called as the **"Field"**, a wise person would read it more like a **battlefield**. Selling is an interaction between the seller and the buyer. Generally, it is heavily loaded in the favour of the buyer at least in the present days.

Let us see the complete process of selling and then marketing before we traverse in the details and intricacies. Selling is one-time activity and when the payment is received the cycle is complete. When the concerted efforts are put in a specific way to ensure that this simple process is repeated again and again between the:

- same product and same buyer
- same product and different buyers,
- different products same buyer
- different products different buyers
- one-time buyers and the repeat buyers
- same area same products
- same area different products

and many such variable combinations it gives a way to one of the complex processes called as marketing of which sales is the integral part. Whatever marketing team does it necessarily has to produce and increase the quantum of sales. These days there is a conscious effort to disassociate from sales. Marketing people do not talk of sales as if it is a job of lesser competence. The most illogical thing to say. Maybe, they are not comfortable about the straight forward and immediately verifiable process of sales.

Many times, many people use sales and marketing as same or equivalent or interchangeable, you have to clearly understand that they are not so. Yes, they are interdependent.

Sales is an effective interaction between a need of a consumer and supply by the seller. We have to ensure that:

- We know how to _find_ what one _needs_
- How to fulfil his _specific_ need
- How to _ensure_ that he gets what he wants or needs

AND

- How to get _equal and fair exchange_ for satisfying his needs, by way of money.

Ideally, things should happen in a slow, deliberate and soft initiation way. But in our scenario, a salesman on his first day is given a pep talk about how his products (he is supposed to sell from today or tomorrow) are the best and the company which is of course _better than the best_. If he is lucky, he may get a semblance of the product training from a person, who is distinctly uninterested, which shows in a profound way. The approach of many companies towards the incoming salesman is questionable. The _trainer_ is convinced that the incoming person is a passing incident so the seriousness is in proportion to the same. Unfortunately, he even mentions the fact to the incoming salesman.

Next day the incumbent is a "Trained Salesman"!

This book is for such persons and it is hoped that they would feel a little more secure after they read this book.

The actual process of the sales is the classical AIDA model, which includes Attention (Awareness), Interest, Desire and Action. AIDA was first developed by E. St. Elmo Lewis as early as 1910. The same can be applied to all categories of products and consumers. Now of this is true why some are better than others? Why when some go, they always get orders? Why then some people are more composed and confident? As Shiv Khera puts it do they do *different things* or do they *do same things differently*.

The differences are working even before the enquiry is generated.

Basic preparation of the salesman: Apart from what is discussed in the chapter You there are some things the salesman has to know.

1. The salesman **must** have a thorough knowledge about his products. This is absolutely **non-negotiable**. The knowledge comes from the trainings, product literature of your company as well as the competition, further reading some relevant books. The practical input of the problems faced and how they were resolved comes from your dealers as well as form the competition.

There is a simple test of this process. The knowledge should be such that whenever the problem is mentioned you should instantly recall the relevant product from your range and its advantage over the nearest product from competition. When you can assert that your product can be a better choice without being hypercritical about the products from competition. Please always remember that we are living in an open ended and handed technology world. You would even find that the products are more or less similar. So, you have to establish the pedigree of your products and their efficacy. Avoid best, cheapest, number one, ways of convincing. Ideally you should be in a state of a "casual" dominance, because of your knowledge. All salesmen worth their salt, sadly know that they spend **less** time to improve their lots before the ball is rolled than the time they spend on the subsequent collection and correction of facts reports.

It helps the salesman to check up his bag. The bag of a salesman is sometimes even more important than anything in his life. His bag must be a complete office in itself. (A check list is given in the appendix.) The bag should have from stapler pins to revenue stamps. More time spent here reduces the pain, agony and dejection at a later stage.

The process of sales is depicted in the figure titled as "the retention of interest", there are three basic steps called as _pre-contact, contact and the post-contact_. We would study

Pre-contact: This is usually a phase of preparation. The better you are here better are the chances of the success. Please collect as much information about your customer you are about to contact.

In case of an industry, you should find out

- The year of the initiation
- Last year's performance
- Percentage of dividend given in the last year

- Any other factory or unit apart from the one you are visiting.
- Is the other unit is already buying your products?
- The frequency and the quantity and the rates offered
- If yes

  - How much and how
  - Do you have order copies?
  - Do you have performance certificates?

  - Are you sure that there were no issues or hassles?

<u>The actual user-</u>

- What type of a person he is?
- Is he a stickler for quality?
- Does he assert himself?
- Is he a good listener?
- Does he have the decision power to place the orders?

<u>In case of a dealer-</u>

- How long is he in the trade?
- How long your company's association with him?
- What is his outstanding payments position?
- Does he promote your products?
- Does he behave with you with respect or he just tolerates your company?
- Does he take pride in the association with you?

In case of a customer (non-Categorised)

- Does he know what he wants?

- Does he have enough money?
- Does he show any specific brand preference?
- Does he believe in listening to you?
- Is he accompanied by his family?
- What category of ABC he belongs to? A or B or C

What you must have observed so far is that a basic guideline is offered to you for you. It is never enough. The complexity keeps on going up or down depending upon your preparations.

Contact: Contacting a customer is the first outside your comfort area task you would be doing. Just like all knowledge outside the swimming pool is useless once you dive in a pool, you would feel very tense nervous and useless. If you would feel so you are a normal human being.

The contact phase is ideally divided into following:

1. Initiation
2. Interest
3. Problem
4. Solution
5. Commercial closing

The process of sales is tested and rated here in this phase. Before we actually study this one must remember that sales call is a professional meeting. He is there for a purpose. **Never ever dilute this focus.**

You should also know that the best sound any man likes to listen to is _his own._ Remember this absolutely clearly. Do not over shadow with your personality aura, smartness, and so-called product knowledge. The inside fact about sales is that the _not so smart,_ and _needy looking_ person is more likely to succeed than the smart and snobbish.

The total time of this process should be usually twenty to twenty-five minutes, unless you are in for a discussion, justification or projects specifications.

1. <u>**Initiation**</u>: This step should never take more than two minutes. The simple purpose is to introduce yourself and talk about any reference if you have. Do not start parroted speeches. Wait and listen. Listen to even the silence. Silence can be a great help to realise the ambience. The décor of the room, the AC temperature, the face of a person can be your friends.

   Apart from a simple introduction the more important purpose is to establish yourself as someone worthwhile to talk to.

   <u>Introduction:</u>

   a. Please learn to introduce yourself in a neat and succinct way. Ideally you should have three or four scripted variations of how you introduce yourself.
   b. Please rehearse in front of a mirror.
   c. If possible, get this activity supervised and corrected by your immediate superior.

   Please remember that you are supposed to know yourself the best. Can anyone else introduce you in a better way than you. No never! I have seen many sales persons who fumble even while telling their names. That is the worst thing you can do to yourself. It creates an absolute poor first impression. Nothing in a sales function is casual. It is directed towards the next step. So, the basic function of the introduction is to create that little bit of curiosity and readiness to listen to what you would have to say. The potential buyer should think "Oh! Seems to be a good guy! Let me listen to him and what he has to offer."

2. **Interest:** The second most important thing is the arousal of interest of the customer in you and your products. So, try to talk to him about himself. Make him talk about what interests him. The most likely item would be his recent success. Ask him a very safe question "How does he do what he does? And still look so cool?" Once he starts talking about him and his achievements as well as his work, he feels that he is in control and he feels good. He feels like talking to you. Next you lead him to talk about his problems if any. If he has how does he get rid of them. Does he have any chronic or persistent problems? Make him talk about his problems. He would give a load of relevant and not so relevant information. Listen to him very carefully, and ask your mind to channelise this flow and come out with the plausible solutions.

3. **Problem:** When the customer shows you his problems and wounds never shirk away. His problems are yours if you want to sell. Be interested in his problems even if you know that _you do not have products_ to cater to his needs. Please listen very carefully. Try to sympathise with him, but never overreact. Whatever you do please do not create an impression that you are superior to the person in front of you.

Next on a piece of a paper do following exercise.

- Identify the problem as exactly as possible.
- Get is confirmed by the customer
- Decide the limits and tolerances acceptable to the

customer.

- Please be clear that you give solutions to a specific, clear and predefined problem. Otherwise, you would find that after you give the solution, the size of the problem grows, just like the nose of Pinocchio.

4. **<u>Solution:</u>** Providing solutions to the problems posed by the customer forms the most important part apart from concluding the deal. This decides the quality of your relationship between you, and your *would be* and even *existing* clients. However, in both the cases the changes or differences are pretty minor. Before you provide a solution to a specific problem you should have done a simple exercise.

ABC LIMITED
Mr. Anand Gupte
NOIDA
22/08/ 2020
Sr.No.
Problem posed
Solutions offered/pending

The sheet should have the name of the company, person of contact, date and place.

One more rule is followed. Never offer solutions in a dictatorial way. At the same time do not appear condescending. Do not for your own sake appear smarter than the client even if you think so. Do not be over bearing. Try to offer solutions with options. Explain the cost benefits of each option. To be able to choose maintains his ego. Once the options are given stop for a moment. Let the person analyse his own situation in the light of the most likely solution. Let that computer of work inside and wait for a printout.

Once the solutions are mentally accepted quite a few things would happen. The most important from your point of view is that you would be a part of the team, along with, your customer which may have to work together for the necessary approvals and /or sanctions. You are a team and imagine with whom, "Your Customer"! What better deal can you ask for?

5.<u>Commercial Closing:</u> Closing is the last lap of the race. You have run nicely. But even in the actual race if you do not run the last lap properly you lose the race. Same here! The proper closing alone decides whether or not you are profitable.

By now you must be ready with a mental offer to be presented to the customer. It always helps writing the offer in the presence of the customer. Make a best offer as a quotation and wait. The customer is on the threshold of the decision which needs backing up by finance. Till now he was happy that he was getting solutions for his problems. Now the <u>scene</u> changes, and he has to think of provision of funds. He may have to take necessary sanctions. If possible, please insist and somehow meet the decision-making person with him. This single step cuts down a lot of time lag and delays. Once the approval is obtained, please insist for an order. If immediate order is not possible at least get a letter of intent.

One last tip!

After you get the order just say good bye and leave the scene as early as possible. Thank them and leave.

By now, are you thinking the different ways you have been handling the process. Did you get any fresh ideas? Please understand that you have to be different if not distinguished from all other salesmen who have parroted their way out of the minds of the customers. You have proved that you are friend, as solution provider, rather than a mere salesman.

Post contact: Once your precontact and contact periods are over, you have to ensure your commitments regarding prices, delivery schedules, and after sales services. The reason is if you somehow keep the right profile, you have developed a contact and you can spare that extra time on some other customer or products. It should be simple but sadly it is not. The details are discussed in the chapter called "the internal selling".

Every salesman who wants to excel in the sales field, should do this post contact activity very seriously. Have checks on what produces best results and then just repeat the process. You would know that you have achieved the level of skills required, by the increase in orders and less of outstanding payments. And if you are lucky even by a promotion.

***

CHAPTER V

THE PURCHASE MANAGERS

As the other side of the coin, you would meet a variety of purchase managers. I also have. They are very typical. They deserve a respect for the simple reason that they allow you to talk, present your products despite of their crack schedules.

Imagine you are a purchase manager, and mentally occupy his chair. Daily, you would be facing a battery of salesmen; some smart others not so smart. On a daily basis. Imagine also listening to following about one hundred times a day, in person or on telephone.

"Sir, my product is the best, the cheapest, and most suitable for your needs. Our services are world class. But you would never need them. Just give us one chance and you would live happily ever after." Just read this for ten times.

Do you realise the pain? Do you feel the pain?

For the sheer torture at the hands of the salesmen I respect these people. I was told that these days the personal encounters are somewhat replaced by emails, and video calls. It must be a great relief. During my interactions with the purchase managers, I came to know some very humorous and some very humiliating stories. Their number is so large that a separate book might be needed.

The purchase manager has to be smart and alert. If he falters a bit and the production is held up, he may receive the classical kick in the butt. The PM faces a double-edged sword all the time. The management theories about the stocks maintaining, the economic order quantity (EOQ), First In First Out (FIFO), or Last In First Out (LIFO), payment terms, credit control, and many such terms can make him as uncomfortable as a cat on a hot roof. How many times we see a desperate PM running from pillar to post to meet the erratic production demands. The assembly line is very threatening. The deadlines are really lethal. Most material is needed on yesterday basis. The planning and all such things are more talked about than followed.

The second factor which is checked by the management is the credit. If anything is bought on cash, it arises quite a few eyebrows. What follows is the scrutiny of the situation and circumstances which prompted such an emergency cash purchase. It is what is the HR calls as a black spot.

The third factor which is under the microscope is the compliance of after sales services by the vendors. It requires a great coordination and it turns out as a thankless job for the PM.

One of the various senior purchase professionals while talking to me said that he likes his job for "The simple reason that he has to meet people who think that they can outsmart him", This one thing always keeps him on his toes and ever alert.

While meeting the sales people the PM also some how finds time for

1. Vendor development
2. Inventory control/ stores management
3. Ordering
4. Purchases at the peak capacities and at the slow down
5. Credit control for the suppliers
6. Deciding correct quantity, quality, price, delivery schedules, contracts. Transports, sourcing both internal and external, and the most important the payment terms favouring the company.

Depending upon the inputs from my colleagues we can have following types of PMs.

1. Those who listen
2. Those who do not listen.
3. Those who know what they want exactly.
4. Those who try to get the best deals.
5. Those who show that they are very open.
6. Those who go by rules
7. Those who bend and break here and there. But are honest.
8. Those who appreciate sales and the efforts going in
9. Those who are straight forward and knowledgeable.
10. Those who are corrupt.

You would say that all sorts are covered here, may be yes or no. they are just like other human beings, but probably overstressed due to factors outside their control. Moreover, purchase is a staff function so other functions like production, finance, marketing try to treat them like not so important and also like a readymade punching bag.

The sales people are absolutely incomplete without this vital factor in the process called selling.

Purchase managers are more relevant in the industrial marketing. There is no dearth of experts in the industry. Steel, cement, power, coalfields and such sectors have many. Every salesman learns a lot from these almost wizards. There are a few who may not buy from you but even then, they teach you a thing or two. They can discuss why the orders were not placed on you. It is suggested that the salesman must find suitable time to discuss things with the PM. He may earn a lot more than many trainings combined at his company.

PMs have little time for incompetence. They inadvertently turn into cynics as they are constantly aware of the threat of getting cheated. Though the functions of the PM remain somewhat similar in all sectors, each sector needs a special expertise to cater to the demanding and exact needs of the production and other departments.

***

CHAPTER VI

INTERNAL SELLING

Internal selling is not a very common term and even the fresh sales people are not aware about this very peculiar phenomenon. The salesman encounters internal selling once he starts getting orders. Every salesman has suffered due to this many times self-destructive process, which has potential to destroy the developed market for a company.

Generally, nobody is careful enough and hence this dirty process with office politics as a supplement is thriving in every company. To understand this peculiar process, we have to go back to the beginning of the salesman's career. After the usual training, and few days of rest-in period the salesman goes in the market with the sole purpose of getting orders. He discovers that whatever training he had been given is inadequate. The market is ruthless and it teaches the real selling. He faces a tremendous pressure from the bosses for completion of the targets, and coverage of area. He somehow finds ways to find, talk, and get orders. Overjoyed he very innocently forwards or submits the orders to the branch or head office, and expects some really smooth processing. Here he faces yet another unexpected and very stark reality which is called the "internal selling"

He is not at all prepared or equipped for this shock. More often than not he finds that the external selling to outside customers is easy when compared to internal selling.

The salesman has a fair idea about the delivery schedules, costs, and accordingly he commits to the customer. Suddenly he finds that the people who should have been on his side are acting very strange and many times he feels like he is an outsider.

Why this happens?

How many sales managers are aware about such a problem in their organizations? If they know what all they do about the same? They have an organization to cope up with diverse issues. They must weigh much more than the lonely salesman.

Once the processing office receives the order it is marked to a department called sales administration department (SAD). The department checks out the order for the discrepancies and other things. It formally accepts or rejects the order. When the order is accepted, an acknowledgement is sent to the party along with tentative delivery schedules. The order is then forwarded to the production department. They produce either fresh goods or supply from the existing stocks. The packed and finished goods are handed over to the despatch department.

In the meanwhile, the accounts department raises the invoice and transporters details are included and the goods are finally despatched. The salesman then collects payments and one cycle of sales is completed. Very simple, isn't it? We should never have any problems in such a simple and clean process. But you would know that even the very simple things when done on a large scale, many times can become messy.

Today one of my friends who is working in a office furniture products company, very *reputed at that*, narrated a very interesting story to me. His monthly target was Rs. Nine lakhs and the quarterly (April May June) target was Rs. twenty-seven lakhs. He placed an order worth six lakhs and thirty-eight thousand and his target was achieved on 15th June itself. He was already in the extra five percent and was making plans for spending the extra money.

At this point, the regional manager walked in the office and the trouble started for my friend. Out of the item for he had collected nearly forty percent were out of stock with no chance of getting them on the assembly line for at least next ten weeks. The regional manager with all his polish and smooth talk and of course, his ever-present laptop had nothing good to say. Further he said that the company would be able to supply only chairs but not the tables for next ten weeks.

My friend was absolutely crest fallen. But he was of the older seasoned stock of hardcore salesman, he reconciled very fast. He got the present stock list. Proceeded to the client and somehow could negotiate for the terms and at the end of the month could still get his extra 5%. Any experienced sales person would be able to identify himself with my friend.

The problem with Indian management is that the influence of the people in the factory or the H/O is exaggerated. In many companies the peon of the MD is more powerful than the managers. The production people have no feeling for what goes on in the market. Ask any production manager, he would always tell that his products are world class, and simply because of this *sole reason* they should be automatically sold. Very strange! The efforts of the production are very visible because of the piling of stocks and because of the money invested. And more often than not they are in daily touch and within hearing distances of the decision-making-unit of the organisation.

As against the salesman is in some god forsaken place doing his best to sell the "World-class" products. He is doing his best but has no witness to bear him out. He is working against all odds. He gets the orders. The effort most likely goes unappreciated, after all the products are world class.

So, when he gets some problems, he has to initiate a process called as Internal selling. As earlier explained, there are many pitfalls between the procurement of the order and getting paid for same.

Sales Administration Department

The acronym for this dept. is very appropriately SAD. Generally, the people here are working overtime to show that they are working. Maybe they are! Let us assume, that a company is getting about hundred orders per day. So, each of the members has his work cut out. The time study shows that each order takes about ten minutes to process. So, you can calculate the load etc. But unfortunately for the salesman they work in the visibility of the marketing managers and they can create an impression that they are the busiest people in the office if not the city. They behave as if each order they process is their own and the salesman is not involved. All salesmen are facing the tussle with the SAD day in and day out.

The usual reasons thrown at the face of the salesman are:

1. Order is not clear.

2. Stocks not available
3. Raw material shortage
4. Order confirmation not received from the party.
5. Power cuts
6. Labour problems
7. Transporter does not accept the consignments.
8. Sanctions from MD for the rates offered cannot be taken as MD is out of country
9. Payment terms not acceptable.

The salesman is involved in convincing /or selling the importance of fulfilling the order. He talks about the importance of the order in the overall plans of the company. He cajoles, deals with soft hands but sometimes he has to threaten to contact the MM or MD. This is a routine affair in the lives of salesmen.

After all this the order somehow reaches the production plant. In the normal times the order gets supplied. But in about thirty percent times the complications set in. the reasons cited are:

1. Production scheduling (or lack of it)
2. Power shortages
3. Lack of manpower
4. Lack of one component, rest everything is available
5. Sometimes sheer callous indifference
6. Apart from the salesman no body in the company is happy for the increase in orders. They see it as additional load.

Let us assume that the order has been supplied and the client rejects the goods on the basis of poor quality. This triggers a new war between salesman and the quality control people. The general attitude of the Q/C people towards the salesman is <u>poor</u> to say the least.

To complicate the matters further if the product is so-called *technical* and the concerned salesman is so-called *non- technical,* then the qc manager takes a quick test on the product knowledge of the salesman on the phone or in person. Very grudgingly he accepts to test the product.

What an insult?

All this time the salesman is trying to cope up with the irritated, livid and wildly abusive customer. He is bound by the procedure in which he has to procure a sample from the customer, and fill in a detailed report. He sends the sample with a report and then the eternal waiting for the reply from the q/c. This is easy when the salesman and the plant is in the same state. But if the plant and the client are in two different states of India, then lot of paperwork is to be attended. This may take a week to a fortnight. By this time the customer is ready to kick the salesman.

After the due delay, a report is sent to the client.

Any guesses?

The report categorically states that the product sample was within the *tolerance limits, and that it conforms to BIS, DIN, ASTM* and a few others. The q/c has successfully washed away his hands. In no way the report helps the salesman and the heat is even more. Here he is with a questionable material firm his company and with a livid customer. Ask any salesman worth his salt he would have a very little good to say about the qc people. (There should be a comprehensive and integrated training in which the production and Q/C people must visit at least one client per month so that a lot of cobwebs would be cleared. Similarly, the sales people should also be made aware about production and Q/C process.)

One more department with whom the salesman has a continuous clash is the accounts and finance. These people behave even bigger than the boss himself. They think that they own the company and accordingly they treat the lesser mortals called salesmen.

Many times, I have tried to analyse the internal hot tussle and have been able to find out some possible solutions.

1. The salesman must be in constant touch with all these departments as his performance depends on their work culture.

2. **He must develop a solid rapport with these people. In fact, he must treat these people as the most important customers. Why? Simply because these are the people he is stuck up with. He cannot change them. If the salesman has some issues with the outside customers, he has a choice, he can find some new customer. He can work with them or dump them. In his own company he has no choice. What can he do?**

3. Always carry gifts for the SAD/and production people.

4. Never step on the toes of even a peon in the head office. You never know he might be the only person when the boss had started the company.

5. Keep very good relations with the drivers, personal assistants, and such people of the MD, MM, or even the FM. They would give you the information which may save you and your job.

6. Develop your image as a good salesman and let people know that you mean business.

7. Pray to God that He gives them some insight of your job.

Once a friend of mine was negotiating a big deal with a government department. The direct demanding office was the DRM, the divisional railway manager. He was convinced about the products but as per their rules he needed a demo and samples at the site. So, he placed a trial order for small quantity, and after the usual checks the final orders would be placed. Please note no FREE samples! My friend was aware about the SAD in his company, and how callously they handle small quantity orders. So, he made a page long justification and further projection of the orders along with the formal order.

After a fortnight nothing happened. He got worried, he talked to SAD, they said that they had despatched the order. As a last resort he spoke to the MD and requested a fast response.

Two days later he received a long letter telling him that the address of the DRM Central Railway had changed and the *poor* courier could not locate the address. We all know that the offices of DRMs etc generally do not change and even if they do, the frequency would be once in a century.

My friend was at the end of his wits. He called the SAD who were protecting the courier as they were getting their money from the courier company. The salesman was on the last priority. He confirmed in writing that the DRM office was **"where it was"** but requested the SAD to send the parcel to his residential address. All this wasted about two more weeks, the order was lost. All because of some callously careless attitude of the SAD people. My friend was disgusted and he quit the company. But now he is more careful.

So, in short, all aspiring and practising salesmen must treat *internal selling* more important than the external selling. Any failure in internal selling can result in a loss of order, loss of face, or even a loss of job. The tussle between the procedure and the on-the-job field decisions would never end. They see the elephants in a different and personalised perspective. Salesman wants to bend some rule just for getting the long-awaited closing of an order. But his effort gains no ground unless the SAD understands the pain of what happens in selling. So far nothing much has changed so the battle is on.

***

Chapter VII

PHILOSOPHY OF SALES

I can already see that very wry smile on your face, as you read the heading of this chapter. You are probably saying to yourself "Come on! What has philosophy to do with sales?" Normally you would be right in saying so in cases of most of the sales people you might have interacted with. But I divide the sales fraternity into two categories as follows:

1. Those who sell because they like to
2. Those who sell because they do not have anything else to do.

In the present post pandemic scenario in our country we find that jobs are hard to come by, the VRS is shifting CRS, where contract employees are slowly but steadily replacing the regular on the roll employees, where many giants in public sector are facing distinct lockout possibilities, where the general atmosphere is a queer mixture of inflation and deflation, where the plum jobs are very rare, where for a job of a peon in a government postgraduates apply, were fresh graduates are mortally afraid to peep in to their future, where the size of Ascent supplement is all time small, where software professionals are queuing for normal menial jobs, the things look bleak.

In such a scenario, people after graduating find that getting a job in the sales field is comparatively easy. No exams, and no grind like the medical, engineering fields entry exams if one wants to start as a salesman. There is no restriction. Probably, because of an easy entry, most people enter this field without knowing much about the same. It is easy!

The entry point is the major reason for the success or failure in the sales job. Chances of people who succeed in this very unforgiving and trying career are higher in case it is a "Chosen" field. Those who fail are generally those, who enter sales as a second or even a third choice. In fact, this may be the demarcating factor between the better and the *bitter salesman*. The process of sales has to be understood and further if possible internalised.

The philosophy of sales can be better understood if the process of sales is properly studied.

<u>What is Sales process?</u>

Classically it is defined as a fair, equal, legal, exchange of goods or services to fulfil one's need or needs against some pre-decided compensation say in terms of money. And as per the real wizard and guru of modern marketing, Philip Kotler the marketing is the efforts put in to generate the repetitive sales of the same product to same or different consumers.

There is a tendency to use these two terms as same or equivalent or instead of each other which is totally wrong. Marketing is more comprehensive as well as integrated process of which sales is a function, albeit n important one. Sales can survive without marketing but it is not vice versa.

So let us start at the basics:

- What do you do when you buy anything?
- What are the factors that make you buy a particular product?
- What is the impact of promotion in your purchase decision?
- What is the role of the opinions you receive from friends, or relatives?
- What is the role of price in the purchase decision?
- What is the part played by the person on the spot (point of purchase)?
- Are you really *sure* that you want to buy a particular product from a wide range of similar products available right in front of you? If *yes* why? Also,

if you are *sure,* are you *sure* for the reasons that make *you sure?*

As per my experience and understanding sale of any product is because of the confidence generated by the salesman for himself first and then for his product.

Let me try to explain by asking you a question!

How often you buy a product from a salesman you do not like or trust? Usual answer would be a NO. The product and its details, utility, after sales service, and even price would cross your mind much later and certainly after your acceptance of the salesman as a decent and sincere person. So, any sale is a direct or indirect reflection of this confidence.

There are three basic components (or more recently referred to as the stake holders) of the sales function.

1. The first and the foremost is you as the customer
2. The product you really want to buy to fulfil your perceived need

3. The person who offers services to provide you the product.

Let us analyse the first component is in some more details.

You: You decide whether the process would be initiated, continued and concluded by the actual payment of money.

So, take out "you" from the sales and the process turns futile without any real objective. Can you imagine playing a football match without a goal post? All twenty-two players and two referees cannot play football without the goalposts. Similarly, always remember that 'you' form the vital part of the process. At the same time, you alone cannot control the process. The reason is that you are one of the many customers. If you decide not to buy it hurts but there are more options. Someone else would buy. So, in such a case the salesman has to find a new house, another door or an organization who would have need for his product.

Product: When you buy a product you are fulfilling one of your many needs. Many times, that is why, even the best of salesmen cannot close a sale as the customer he is talking to is not interested in that product at that particular moment of time. There are two types of customers. The first type is the one who knows exactly what he wants and the second who does not know what is needed by him. The first is relatively easy to deal with. If you have the right product then it would be bought rather than sold at a full price. Second type would be slightly tricky. Here the salesman has to work a lot more. He has to identify the need, then suggest a solution, then recommend the product. The sales occur subsequently. Because the customer is in doubt he listens to all salesmen from all available companies and gets even more confused and lands up with a product that may not be at all suitable.

A simple advice for the customers as to how they should decide:

- **Identify the need.**
- **Classify the need.**
- **Crystalise the need.**
- **Do a short cost benefits analysis on need versus the cost of fulfilling the need.**
- **Arrive at a conclusion.**
- **Then search for a brand.**
- **Then simply buy.**

The person who tries to fulfil your need i.e., the salesman.:

Salesman is a person who most people underrateandunderestimate, or even ridicule. How often have you closed your door on the face of a salesman? Have you ever thought that in spite of all insults, derogation, ridicule how salesmen still achieve their goals or targets?

The logic is simple. A customer for any salesman is a number. The customer is a part of yes and no game. When a salesman is moving in the market following things would be more or less constant.

1. His target in numbers like so many pieces per month
2. Territory is constant.
3. Total number of available customers at any given point of time

So, what should he do? He has to find his averages. Suppose he finds that out each ten persons contacted two would buy his products. And his target is, say, 100. Then it simply means that he has to contact five hundred people. Now instead of finding out how he would find five hundred people if he starts analysing why eighty percent say no, he would be in a serious crisis. All he has to do is change the focus to those who say yes, and be happy for those who say yes. If he manages to focus on yes, he would be happier, would have better focus, and would have more chances of becoming successful and staying successful. Sales is a repetitive process and this fact should never be forgotten. It is the intent to work than intelligent to work which succeeds in sales.

Initially in this chapter we described two types of salesmen.

The first type which has people who sell because they like to sell and generally, they follow the proven and well-travelled path of more contacts result in more sales. They do it knowingly or inadvertently. They do their jobs with pleasure and a smile on their face.

The law of averages is for the second types who sell because they could not do anything else. And presently also they nothing else to do. If they inculcate the habit of following the rule of average and start to contact more people when it <u>hurts them the most</u>, they would start producing results. And believe me success is the biggest possible motivator.

Second important thing the salesman should always remember is to contact people with whom they do not feel comfortable. Most salesmen while away their precious time in chatting and gossiping chatting with the customers who make them comfortable. These customers may never buy the products and hence the salesman would categorise these calls as the follow -up calls in his daily sales reports.

These calls are one of the root causes in the fall of performance. The supervisors who are smart insist that at least two new customers must be contacted on a daily basis. The logic in this is simple as any thing else in sales. As per the wise men 'If a product is exposed to a substantial sample of prospective buyers the sale of product would follow a set pattern of yes and no over a period of time.' The pattern would have variations and hence a smart supervisor is necessary. So, if a salesman knows and understands this rule, he is not likely to be discouraged by a barrage of '*no*' es in the market. But does this alone suffice? A big no!

The salesman has to essentially know and internalise following things.

1. Personal appearance.
2. Product knowledge.
3. Knowledge about the customers and their needs.
4. Complete trust in his ability and his products.
5. Act in genuine enthusiasm.
6. Know his own pattern of percentages of getting <u>a yes and a no.</u>

It can be safely concluded that if a salesman knows his customer fully, and is prepared to try out his percentage principle, he should find himself in more happy situations and should be able to maintain good posture.

The salesman should also know that the process of sales is and <u>equal exchange</u> between the need and the price. So ideally, he should not be begging for a sale. On the other hand, he has to also know that he has to be decent, humble and a facilitator to the customer. He must bear in his mind:

"For every customer, who does not buy from him, he can find an alternate customer, but so can every

customer find an alternate product and a salesman in whom he can trust more.”

Till such time a workable balance is maintained selling remains a funny and satisfying profession.

***

<u>Chapter VIII</u>

<u>Boss/ Bosses/ Bossism</u>

In any field, one needs constant guidance and mentoring to remain on the right course and be productive as per the expectations of the management. It is accepted that without a mentor or a guru you are more likely to go down. **“Binguru Gyan kahan se pau”** very appropriately describes the relationship between a guru and a pupil.

While we acquire our education many teachers, guides, mentors and coaches form us from outside and from inside. During this stage, the person is young and immature so he rarely understands the effort that goes in. The proverbial putty is being shaped by many sculptors. When the formal education is over (and done with) one starts to think and work about his career one absolute fact surfaces. It tells him that whatever knowledge he gained is a mere gate pass to an enormous arena called “life”. In a professional life whether one is successful or not, greatly would depend upon what sort of boss he gets in his first job. You may talk to many successful people in diverse professions and would find one common thing that they all had a boss who taught them right things, in a right way and at right times. The initial stage becomes the solid foundation for a successful life.

Let us understand this special person, with whom every body has to interact. One has to be alert in his presence, listen to him with rapt attention and even keep him happy and perform as per his expectations.

Boss to me is a **"Better Organised Superior Soul"**. We try to describe an ideal boss. An ideal boss for whom the juniors are ready stretch beyond limits or more fashionably stop a bullet for him. If you have such a person to work, most of your problems do not even germinate. So, you start thinking about the attributes of a person for whom you would willingly stop a bullet. What is the first that comes to your mind, the second or the third and so on and so forth.

1. That he should be a good human being. Think about this for a while. A good human being is available almost everywhere, but not all of them cannot be good bosses. But this is the first thing that comes to our mind. Though it is not enough by itself.
2. That he should be knowledgeable.
3. That he should know where he is going
4. That he should be sincere and not a phoney.
5. That he should be a team-man'.
6. That he should be approachable.
7. That he should be balanced
8. That he should not be a credit monger
9. That he should be fair to all involved.
10. That he should be strict but he should give a fair trial to a person failing in his initial tasks
11. Absolute sound character as far as money and women are concerned.
12. That he should be able **to do**, what you are supposed to do, in a much better way than you.
13. Lastly, he must be a "Practise first preach later".

You may add your own as this list is not complete. When your list is ready try to rate your present boss on a scale of one to ten and if possible, show it to him and watch his response and his behaviour later on. This single thing would tell you many things about him.

During my entire career, I met only one person who used to give us a format called "Boss Appraisal Format". He had a tabulated format where in we were just supposed to tick. More surprisingly, the corrections suggested were adopted by this wonderful Person.

The discussion here should be enough to give you an idea about what an ideal boss should be. The further part would tell you what you would find in the practical future life of a salesman.

So, a classification is offered:

1. **Let us do it type:** this type of the bosses is highly educated, very sober, and believe in delegating. They know exactly what they want, and more often than not, have even the roles written for their junior colleagues. They would help quite a few times if you are sincerely putting in the efforts.

2. **Phoney over-dressed type:** Usually you would come across this type in advertisements or white goods sector. They can be good but the percentages are more towards the worse. They are more concerned about their looks than the products or the market. Generally, they are not very well received. The market responds in its own inimitable way, which means that they are ridiculed. If you are not sure about whether a person is a phoney or not all you have to do is to watch their eyes. Their smile hardly ever reaches their eyes. They would never remember anything you told them. They would over react and put all the blames on you that too in front of the dealers or customers. They would promise things which they you know can never be fulfilled. They have

a lens ready to find faults in everything and everyone around them. If you are in a town and he is from a metro then you would listen to the insufficiencies hundred times in one day. One such person used to be my boss.He was a pain everywhere. When he came to Nagpur (which is a fairly big city, 10th largest in India) we were having a lunch, in a three-star ITDC approved restaurant. He dissected each dish to such a level that I lost all my appetite. He ate everything on the course, but he compared and complained about everything. He also told me "See if you have to have a chicken clear soup nothing beats Sheraton, sizzlers only in Kolkata, and fish only in Amritsar." I thanked God that this fellow was not working internationally. A thought crossed my mind. If this fellow would be half as fastidious towards the job as he was for his food our company would be making double the sales and the profit. But then he was the boss!

3. **English only type:** This type is a sure disaster if you are working in company which caters to rural markets in India. In quite a few markets in UP, MP, Maharashtra, and even in Gujrat the dealers hardly give any response leave aside positive to English. At the back of such bosses there is a constant funny commentary going on. The worse part is their English as a language is very limited. They speak with horrible accents and their written communication is pathetic. To tackle this type, you have to be diplomatic enough to tell him that the dealers are not as good as him so he should speak in Hindi or the local language.

4. **Amateur Psychologists type:** This is one of deadliest species of the bosses. Because if they conclude that you are not their type your career in that company is over. Be very careful of how you behave in front of these

people.

For example

- If you laugh a lot - You are casual.
- If you talk a little loudly - you are arrogant.
- If you sit resting in the

back of a chair - You are laid back.

- If you cross your hands - You are negative
- If you wear dark shirts - You have criminal tendencies

It goes on and on...

It is really surprising that these people easily condemn good, decent, hard -working people for them. Even Sigmund Freud would have been more careful about such statements, but not these people. These people are overly interested in the family background of a person. If they come to know that some person five generations ago had some minor issues, they would immediately start looking for symptoms in your behaviour. All your accomplishments have no bearing. It would help this type to read in depth about body language, kinesics, and psychology before hanging their people.

The first thing a student of psychology learns is not to study any behavioural pattern is absolute isolation. There are simpler explanations available for actions of people than the phobia, mania, and psychosis.

5. **Bulldozer Divers:** This is the most common type in the Indian scenario. They would shout, scream and always ready to throw a tantrum at you asking you to do what

nobody has done from the inception of the company. They expect you to do but if you ask for how they would not know. Very loud both in appearance and sound. You have to develop your own discounting factors when you deal with such a boss. If you are keen and observant enough you would talk to your seniors and find out whether he is a barking or a biting boss.

6. **All are fools in this company:** This type is usually available in the regional or zonal offices of the companies. These would constantly tell their juniors about how he improved the lots in the company by confronting the MD or even better the chairman and telling them the mistakes in the company. You better do not believe him until you see the truth in the all India/ national level meetings. Here you would notice that nobody in the top management ever notice him. You would further observe that he would accept everything the top boss says and that he would contradict everything he promised you and he would stop at nothing in becoming the best available_stainless-steel spoon_ in the meeting.

7. **All core no polish:** These types are generally available on the shop floor type industries. These people are simply superb. They would anything to meet the targets. They know their team very well. They fight for their people and the management knows that this is a _real man_ who is not bothered about anything except the core work. They get a lot of respect. People look up to them. All organizations should treat them as the real assets. I have seen a few of this type. Even today I wonder how they produced without a blemish and met the deadlines without any failures. You would rarely see such a person in the comforts of AC. You would find him toiling with

the machines and with grease on his hands.

8. **When I was in States/ Europe/ Japan type:** There are plenty of this type in today's situations. They begin and end with their monotonous routine.

"In States they do it in this way. Here it is rubbish." They would ask for everything but would rarely achieve anything worthwhile. If caught with this type you take a deep breath and bear somehow and sincerely wish to God to send these people back to where they came from.

9. **Appreciative:** This is a rare commodity. Probably most conventional bosses believe that any appreciation reduces the zeal to work. They have never believed that a simple pat on the back can double the output. "You did a good job, keep it up" is the real energy for the people in the organization. Like all good things the appreciative boss is also very rare almost like a black pearl.

10. **Cool as a cucumber type:**This is also a rare type. But not as rare as the previous one. They have a way of absorbing shocks, which is contagious and works very well for the team. In times of distress and duress they would simply say "Okay, forget what has happened. Let us concentrate on the future. What can we really do now? Do you need any special approvals etc? in the long run they always finish the race with flying colours. Not only that they also create a strong team.

I hope you have a fair idea of what you would be getting in your jobs. The list can be further stretched, but that would redundant.

One story would explain the behaviours and what can be waiting for you.

In one of the companies, I worked a funny situation developed. Three bosses converged on me as I was the number two. One was a regional manager; one was the out going branch manager and the third was the incoming branch manager.

As usual at the behest of the RM it was decided that an announcement of the change in management would be made by him at the dealer cum press conference. I was told to arrange the same. Time was 2 PM! Somehow by seven thirty in the evening everything was arranged. A special venue, preparation at the venue, power point presentation was ready. It went very well and the dealers and press went home happy.

The actual fun started after the event. I was shocked when the RM told me that press release must have only his photo with the information. The outgoing BM came and told me that he alone is important and only he should appear in the photographs. The incoming BM who would be my immediate boss for the next few years was even more candid. He told me that photograph should naturally include him alone. I knew that I was in a hopeless situation. I was thinking furiously but nothing seemed worthwhile.

Then suddenly a flash came to my mind. I asked my photographer friend to take a professional snap of the new model to be launched, along with flowers in the background. That was the only photograph which appeared in the press release. And nobody could complain. I could hardly believe that the senior as in designation and age could be so petty minded. It was big lesson for me and I learnt *how not to behave* as a manager.

Bossism: One very interestingconcept one must understand if one has to survive, grow and reach the top of the ladder in Indian management scenario. For that matter in anything and anywhere in the world. The concept of bossism!

There are many perceptions going around when you utter the word boss. The most popular one is the one poster saying "The boss is always right". Everybody except the boss enjoyed the monkey in the poster. You must have seen the one if not then just go to nearest Archies gallery and see.

Is the boss always, right? If he is or he is not? Does it really matter?

Seemingly, the boss is always right matters, because the concept of bossism originates here. The worst part is further that most bosses seriously believe in this statement. If are an operating boss you may not answer to me but you may in your mind answer.

Bossism is more prominent in the government or public sector. Ask any executive engineer or a plant manager he would tell you incredible, as well as bizarre stories. They have to cope up with their bosses doing many things outside the purview of their job profile. As if the bosses are not enough their wives are added as a bonus. If your plant in Banaras, guess what is most liked by the lady and the lord! A silk saree to begin with, a VIP darshan, boat rides, and so many other things. Same story can happen in Mumbai, Pune, Hyderabad, and almost all cities. Average expenses can run in to thousands of rupees and even then, the boss and *his boss* are not satisfied.

You can see many scenes at the airport where, the garlands, the bottles, the fake smiles, the extra humility, and the hidden disgust tell the inside story. Are they acceptable, funny or sickening?

One simple theory about the boss! If the boss has to tell that he is the boss then he is not. He may be a mere senior person because he was born earlier than you. He may be a person seating in the chair by fluke. In the minds of his employees, he is simply a nuisance and a professional evil which has to be tolerated.

Does it mean that all bosses are either good or bad? No, it would not be black or white but more in grey shade. And as it goes in the other activities of life statistics takes over. No boss can be the ideal variety. He may have some good, some acceptable qualities. On the other side of spectrum, he may have some shortcomings. Also, various situations would affect his performance. You can always rate him on a scale of 1 to10, and derive your own conclusions. Best way to do is to imagine that you are the boss. Mentally seat in his chair try to think like him. Most of the things would be sorted out by asking simple questions and finding solutions. Many times, you would be surprised that how close you are to him in the thinking.

Getting a good boss is as important like getting a good wife or husband. In both cases, adjustments and flexibility are needed. One who adjusts faster benefits faster in both cases. A man has to accept that he works with two bosses. The boss at the workplace may turn out as a less dangerous option as you can change him by changing the job. So, enjoy at both places while you can.

As a person from marketing, I would always prefer a boss who has some basic understanding in front line selling. You would be surprised the ease with which you can work with such a person. He would be sympathetic, and strict but he would stand by you. Ask any active sales person "What frustrates you most?" very often he would tell like debriefing to a non-sales boss. One of them told me that *non sales and nonsense* go hand in hand.

So far, we have tried to describe and analyse the very significant part in the organization.

One more story relating to a *Number One* man in one of the largest companies in India, now expanding very fast in States and Europe.

He is a middle-aged restless man, very graceful, soft spoken and generally believing himself and his people. Guess what does he do on a daily basis? In his huge chamber which has a round table and few chairs, he has a routine. The room is at the top floor and has full glass on one side. He has a recliner called in Hindi as *aaramkhurchi*. He seats in this chair playing with ideas, notions, concepts and possibilities. He says that he lives in the future. At least ten years ahead, and visualises what his company would look like, work like, in the future. He likes to paint the future with all possible colours. He is at peace and at his creative best when he in in the chair.

When an idea is germinated, he would call all relevant stakeholders, and have a brainstorming session. No bars type. Many ideas were a waste of time but quite a few finally got converted and still evolving which makes this as the brand leader and social leader. Most certainly and importantly it is not the end but just a plain milestone in a well-planned journey.

Do you think your boss resembles to the described version in any single way? If yes, consider yourself, as the lucky one. Very... very lucky at that!

Please remember that even if you know all the interesting information about your boss it does not actually help you. Between you and your boss it is always you who would have to change, adjust, alter, edit and ensure that you stay in the organization. you have to find the golden mean, where you are more acceptable to your boss. Rest everything including the customers, market come a distant second. As today most organisations select very average workers, who have lesser skills but are more prone to take things lying down.

You would be well placed if you learn from each of your bosses what should be done and what should not be done. At least in the future your staff would be happy.

<u>Life time tips for salesmen</u>

<u>Check list for a professional salesman</u>

Every salesman should check for the following in his bag and /or laptop.

1. **<u>Office stationery.</u>**

- Large letterheads
- Small letterheads
- Continuation sheets
- Order booking and order confirmation formats
- Quotations formats
- Envelopes small and large
- Product literatures preferably a file
- Product price lists
- Comparison of his products with the nearest competitors
- Certifications like BIS/IS/ ASTM etc
- Important order copies for references.
- Product manuals
- Authority letters if any required
- Identity papers
- Rough pads
- His diary
- Receipt books
- Income tax clearance certificates

2. <u>Office accessories</u>

- Pens blue /black / red
- Stapler with pins
- Small 6 inches' scale
- Calculator
- Cello tape
- Gum bottle or tube
- Sealing wax
- Candle with match box
- Company seal if required for sealing quotations
- Postage stamps/ E-mail IDs/ fax numbers
- Revenue stamps for pre-receipts
- Circular stamp of the company

3. <u>General</u>

- Railway time table/airlines schedules
- City maps if visiting a new city
- Medicine box he should be aware of his needs. Usually anti allergents, medicine for headaches, common cold, stomach upsets. Actually, you should get a proper advice from your family doctor and as per the same the emergency kit must be prepared. A working day lost due to bad health can be very costly.

4. <u>Credit cards and cash</u>

The idea is simple. You should never come back to your office for collecting something which you ought to have in the first place as a regular item in your bag.

***

<u>Diary</u>

As earlier mentioned in this book your habit of maintaining a diary or not can create a run of the mill salesman or an extraordinary one. Diary is a habit which a few lucky ones naturally have but most have to acquire the same. Chronological listing of whatever happens around you can empower you. Also, it is admissible as evidence in the court of law.

It is suggested that any salesman who is serious and committed to his job MUST never retire for the day before he enters his day in the diary. It would never take more than fifteen minutes- *if you maintain on a daily basis*- to finish this task. As in the case of all small and avoidable chores it is very tempting to postpone it for tomorrow, which never comes. Even a single day delay can make it go for ever. The power comes from the regularity of the habit and not from you actually write. You may miss a point or two but it does not matter, as is covered in next few days.

Once you decide to write a diary you should better learn to writing it effectively. After a lot of trial and errors a format is suggested. But it is not the best. You should customise for your own needs.

1. **<u>Inside cover page (First):</u>** All addresses/ mobile numbers with codes/ Emails/ details of Head Office and other offices. Residence numbers of your colleagues. Your emergency numbers.
2. **<u>Inside cover page (last):</u>** All telephone numbers of your clients, dealers, professionals, professionals, newspapers, ad agencies and even friends and advocates.

Your diary should be in such a way that when you refer to it the person in front should accept what you say. It should be a record you can trust.

Sample page from diary

Place:

Date:

Day:

Appointment Discuss with

1. 1. Name: Matter

2. 2.

3. 3.

4. 4.

5. 5.

Do not Forget

1. Last date of Tenders etc.

2. Monthly meeting

3. Air sales service promises

4.

5.

Telephone to Attend Matters On

1. 1.

2. 2.

3.

Today's Events Matters Brought

& Personal Notes: Forward to:

New Contacts Made

(Very important as it creates new business)

New Referrals 1.

2.

Summary

Today's Sale:

Today's Collection:

Cumulative Collection:

SHORT AND SWEET

PLEASE remember following forever:

- Bank accepts **only** cash /cheques/ demand drafts/ NEFT / RTGS
- Projection of sales is a tool **not money**.
- How many **new** customers you contacted today?
- Have you asked for any **referrals**?
- Analyse the order before celebrations. Are **you making any Money?**
- We do business for **earning profits.**

Who is a satisfied customer?

He buys again and again. Repeats orders.

Buys other products of the company.

Talks favourably to Ohers about you, your products and about your company.

Pays less attention to competitor's advertisements and promotions.

Simple but most effective report

Today's sale =

Cumulative sales =

Today's collection =

Cumulative collection =

Rest everything is an effort to accomplish the above.

Things you should always remember as a salesman

1. You are not the only one who thinks smart. There are many others. More so in your own category of products and services.
2. If the order value is more never go alone. Always hunt in pairs.
3. Always listen first. Let the customer talk as he knows the best about what he wants.

4. Try to be different than the typical boring salesman.
5. Prepare yourself, separately for each individual customer. Till it becomes a habit.
6. See things. Ambience around the customer can tell you much more than what he actually tells you.
7. Ease the customer into a need.
8. Be clear, concise and correct.
9. Use pause. Never prompt any action. Never hurry him for taking a decision. Never ever say 'It is a tough time etc'
10. Never restart your sales discussion or pitch once you have reached the closing stage.
11. Always ask for money.
12. You put value on your products. If you feel they are worthy or worthless then they are.
13. Appear sincere, knowledgeable, and straight forward.
14. Do not give an "over smart" or a stuffy impression to your customer.
15. In some product lines you need a partner. Always hunt in pairs. If your partner complements you, you have a better chance to be more successful.

***

Preface

<u>**Why this book?**</u>

In the formal management education, I never realised that I would have to unlearn many things which I was then learning with a lot of effort, money, and other resources. Yes, you can add exertion also. Then Philip Kotler was the last word in sales and marketing and even today he alone rules supreme. Any serious reader should get his queries answered if he reads it with some patience. His book deals mainly with classical marketing problems and dogmas which Indians find slightly alien. There are many other books for those who are willing and ready to put in some time.

After about forty years in sales and marketing as well as training, I thought I should share my experiences in simple language to those who are thrown to wolves without any real training. I hesitated before I shared my desire with my friends, about writing a book, they were not sure as to why. One of them was forthright and asked me 'Why this Book'? so I thought seriously and I explain as below.

<u>The first</u> reason to write this book is to provide answers to some of the doubts in the minds of those who choose to be sales and marketing professionals, with a stress on the practical aspects of the process.

<u>Secondly</u>, this book may serve the purpose of an initial "On the Job" training kit. This is a book for the starters in the field as well as for those who have spent some uneasy time in the field, somehow by fluke achieved some results but presently in a state of amazed inertia and in a constant mental debate whether they are in the right field or not.

<u>Thirdly</u> for those who have a formal training in management, but suddenly are extremely uncomfortable because they find a huge difference between actual and anticipated scenario, they would find this book a reassuring help.

This book intends to help all those selling people to sustain the pressures of selling, supervision, and targets. They would come to know that there is not much difference between them and the successful ones. The little difference they would find would be "that little extra effort at a right time".

There have been many theories which try to tell us about why a product sells or why not. Even after a hundred years in formal management education nobody has come anywhere near for a readymade, easy to consume capsule that would tell us about why a product sell. In the very typical, exclusive and diverse Indian scenario one is classically at the end of his wits and tries his own ways.

This book shall also try to emphasize on one simple fact, that most sales people have highly prejudiced ideas about fairness of life or vice versa. A.J. Cronin said that life is no straight and easy corridor where one can travel free and unhampered. He further said that life is a maze of alleys and passages and each such passage is separate lesson in learning.

Very sincerely put this book tries to decipher between the line's messages, which are most of the times missed either by design or default. All consultants, gurus, books, and even the teachers say that a marketing person needs to be smart, but rarely enough they talk about the key to smartness. This book would try to tell what is that one has to do to become smart. When you shall read this book, you would realise that you can relate with a lot of what it says.

You may even find a solution to your chronic problems. It also intends to provide some fine tuning to people in advanced stages of sales careers.

Every salesperson has to somehow remember that whether successful or not his day would remain same. To be in the market every day, putting behind what happened yesterday, believing in the process and doing same things again and again is his lot. It is up to him whether he does it with a smile or a frown or even a grimace. Whatever else you learn or do under some unwanted influence is simply an illusion.

I would like to cite one simple example. All marketing people need to have a diary and maintain it. How many really do it? How many would like to, but cannot. In this book I have given in details about how a sales and marketing person should keep records. They would help the average sales person to become an outstanding variety.

At the end, if this book starts a process of self-evaluation in the minds of all those who matter and even if lives of a very few salespeople improve by a bit, I shall consider the purpose of the book is fulfilled.

***

Acknowledgements

I express my heartfelt gratitude to all who have encouraged me to write.

I acknowledge with pleasure the interest shown by my friends, colleagues and fellow salesmen. The continuous followup was the catalyst for writing.

I thank my family for supporting me in those difficult moments when things were not looking rosy.

Index

CHAPTER ONE

YOU

YOU

In any walk of life, in any activity of life if you want to be successful, remember YOU form the most important and vital ingredient. Everything minus "You" is virtually useless. The irony is that in most cases you do not know this simple fact. In exceptional cases maybe you know but the significance is apparently lost on "You".

I implore you to realise that unless *you wish* to be successful, this or for that matter any other book would be rendered useless. So, before you start reading this book in a casual way take a very serious and close look at you, both "outer you and "inner you".

<u>What do you think about yourself?</u>

Do you like what you see in the mirror? If yes you have a chance, if you do not like what you see in the mirror you are in a serious problem. Have you ever analysed as to why you do not like what you see? What part of you like and what you do not? I would ask you a simple question. Please answer as truthfully as you can.

Have you come across any other person who is like you? (Even in the cases of identical twins!) The answer should be a big NO.

Now stop for a second, take a deep breath, and start thinking about you. You have not seen any person like you because are an *exclusive edition* created by the God. If He so desired, he could have easily created millions like you, and you could have been one of the clones. But that is not the case. The reason is what you can do nobody else can. The point is to make you realise that you are in this world for some special reason and you are supposed to leave a lasting imprint on the canvas of the world. It may be anything and, in any field, but always remember that you are special.

Whatever is the reason which makes you think that can be a successful marketing/ sales person can be a great help to both of us. This is the primer which would help in creating a new You.

One of my bosses used to say that there are two types of people. One who can sell and the other who cannot. I partially agreed with him as I felt that there is third type of people who does not know they can sell.

The first category of the people is those who inadvertently follow the golden rules of selling, they do all the right things, follow all the "Do's" and without any apparent efforts are successful in sales. For such people this book might serve as a refresher course and they would be able to relate with many things said in the book.

The book is specifically for those who are shy, cannot sell (or think that they cannot sell) and most likely are in selling activity because they could not find anything else.

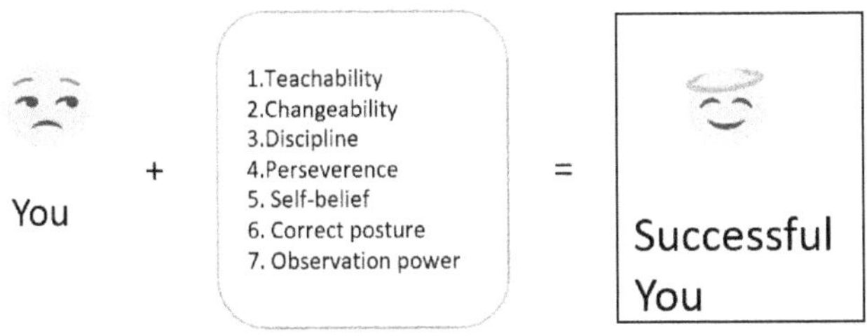

Change You

The "outer You"

You are tall or short, fair or dark, smart or simple, male or female, good and smart talker or not so smart talker, qualified or average, extrovert or introvert, so please be rest assured that you can be very successful in sales as a career. There are thousands if not millions in each of the category, who are very successful, so why not you?

Let us begin at the basics.

1. **Turnout -** As you are aware this is a military term and most of us have heard this when we were at the parade ground of NCC. Have you anytime thought why the NCO gave so much on the correct turnout? Let us begin at the top:

- Are you well groomed?
- Are you clean-shaved? Or with the routine stubble?
- Is your breath fresh?
- Do you smell good?
- Are you wearing a decent business shirt?
- Are your trousers matching to your shirt?
- Are you wearing a correct sized belt?

- Are you wearing a neatly polished pair of shoes? Preferably black and formal!
- Are your socks fresh?
- If you are required to wear a neck tie is it of the colour of the trouser?

Each of the above ten steps, is interlinked which would result in either a well-dressed person or a shabby person. Each step like the shoes, belt, adds to your get up. This sort of dress code increases your self-esteem and confidence. And of course, it adds dignity to your profile.

These days a lot of people are wearing spectacles. May be because of the TV or mobiles. Not many of us attach any importance to what sort of frame we select, we treat this aspect in a casual way. This is true with salesmen. Please check up. Do you realise that the spectacles are right up on your face, which is the most visible and creates the first impact on the people? *Wrong* spectacles on a *rightly dressed* up person can negate the impact. So, spend some time before you select the frame and the lenses.

So much talk about the dressing up brings out a natural question. Who is a well-dressed person? Luckily there is no thumb rule here, but there are many guidelines. The important thing is whether you are able to carry what you wear. There is an aspect of overdressing and low profile. We would understand this by following example.

Suppose, you are at a party, where you meet your friends, associates and clients. You had a good time and gone home. Next day in the morning there is usual talk about the party. A colleague asks you "Hey, do you remember Mrs. Sharma, and what she was wearing yesterday?" Now, if you remember she wearing a cream and black Banarasee saree, a contrast sleeveless blouse, a matching Bindi, a purse and all her ornaments, then the conclusion is simple. She was apparently overdressed. If she was more properly dressed then you might have said "She was looking great, wearing something rich and decent." The point here is that people should remember you as neatly and decently dressed person rather than your entire attire. Remember that you dress up to enhance your personality. People should never remember you as a *dressed-up doll* or a *dandy* person.

The basic purpose is to create a favourable first impression enabling a decent nonverbal communication.

Ladies, if you are reading my book, please forgive me for not dwelling on the topic of your clothes. I know my limits and so I do not dare to teach you anything. However, if you really want to learn then I suggest that seek guidance from any decently dressed lady you know and get some tips. As it is ladies have an inherent knack of knowing what suits them or not.

Remember, the best judge of your dress is inevitably you, yourself. As earlier said well-dressed is anything you wear which makes you feel confident. As a precaution, before you step out of your home, please spare a minute in front of a mirror. Ensure that everything is in place. Once you are sure of your dressing up, you can move out of the real purpose of actual action.

***

The Inner "You"

The inner "you" is the part which is extremely important in making or breaking you. The inner "you" is very personal as against the outer you. The outer you can be shaped or reshaped by instructions or practice more easily than the inner version. The inner you can be improved but it takes more time and even more serious teacher. There are many diverse inputs for the inner you and you must read some serious books on this topic. However, as far as the purpose of sales and marketing you should have following characters.

- Self-respect
- Confidence in the products you wish to sell
- Knowing exactly what you want
- A built-in process of continuous evaluation
- Sincerity and discipline
- Long term relation building rather than a short-term temporary gain.

There can be many more, but these would build you up and prepare you for a long-term success. Please understand that the process of sales is relatively simple. The repetitive nature makes it very taxing and affects the psyche of a person. Moreover, it has a component called a customer very unpredictable, erratic and many times just very taxing for the salesman. In any other activity of life, a person gets a workable experience in a couple of years, which helps him throughout his life. He can relax in the shadow of some specific intelligence. Not so in sales. Day after day, week after week, month after month and year after year he spends his time running after some improbable if not impossible targets. Whatever has been done in the last day, week, month or year is done with and it is of no relevance. Every day is fresh. Just imagine you doing same grind for thirty years and you would get the picture. Moreover, in a country like India, if you *sell* anything it is because of the quality of the products, reputation and the goodwill of the company, but when you do not perform it is only because you are incompetent. We would deal with each aspect in some detail.

1. **Self-respect:** The self-respect stems from thefact that you like yourself and you like what you do. You can very rarely feign self-esteem. There is no artificial self-respect. A person with correct self- respect can always be a good salesman, as he knows his own limits of bowing down. He also understands that selling is ideally an equal and fair exchange of goods and services. Self-respect can be ego or self-esteem. This is a highly volatile and readily perishable. One has to take special care to keep it alive and succeed in sales. Self-respect can be ego or self-esteem. This is a highly volatile and readily perishable. One has to take special care to keep it alive and succeed in sales.

2. **Confidence in products you sell:** when you join any company you are told that the products are world class. The prices and service are no issues. Very soon after a few encounters with the customers and competitors, the sheen starts wearing off.

Here a smart salesman should develop his own scale of ratings. Each product (in a multi products company) should be rated on a scale of one to ten. He can have his own parameters or he can take help from his supervisors. By doing this exercise he can have a correct product mix and can have a rational and correct approach to his product range. Remember customers prefer those salesmen who have a rational and reasonable approach than those who just say their products are the best.

1. **Knowing exactly what you want:** Apart from selling this applies to each aspect of your life. When you at

least know what you want you stand on a sound footing. You have an idea of the probable outcome right in the beginning. It is suggested that you must carry weekly, monthly and yearly "what I want" cards with you. Your actions would be more balanced and more result oriented in your sales routines.

2. **Inbuilt process of continuous evaluation:** This is a real separator between the good, the better and the best salesmen. A mature salesperson must remember quite a few facts, such as his performance for the current month and the year. He must have meter like tendency towards the positives and the negatives around him. The events, the environment, the competition, and all such factors which may affect his routine. He must ask himself a question on a daily basis, which is "Am I where I should be?"

3. **Sincerity and discipline:** A person need to be sincere if he wants to be successful in anything he plans to do. More so in sales! If he has to meet someone, he has to follow the clock. If he has to be in a particular place he must be there. Irrespective of the response he gets from the market he has to maintain his routine. Please understand that the salesman can be rarely monitored by anybody except he himself. These days some companies have started the *minute to minute, place to place* monitoring by mobiles, which is one of the worst things for the sales force and the organisation. The inner drive to excel is generated by the self-discipline. And the discipline starts TODAY, so never plan it for tomorrow.

4. **Long term relationship building approach than temporary gains:** If youare sincere, disciplined and have something better to offer you can be assured of success. More often than not the trust created by the salesperson

results in orders than the typically promoted factors like price, quality and others.

Each customer should be made to feel like a very special and valuable person. The approach from a salesman should be more to solve the problems and clearing the bottlenecks rather than merely pushing for products. Continuous providing of good services, advice, suggestions would always generate repeat orders. And repeat orders is the basic aim of the marketing and sales. The thumb rule is that one satisfied customer is equal to five new one-time buyers. The efforts are less the trust is more.

***

CHAPTER TWO

Every one is a Salesman! Are you?

Every one is a salesman! Are you?
Check out

Conventional marketing is a very big and complex activity and most of the common people find it beyond their comprehension. People have some notions, but the all-important clarity is lacking. We hear people talking about marketing as a process, which someone else is supposed to do and they underline that they are not the part of the same. Some people specifically disassociate with marketing, proudly saying that it is not their cup of tea. The declare that they cannot sell. This statement is very amazing and let us analyse why.

Do you realise that you are a part of a very intelligent species which thrives in a society, and has successfully survived the demands of the very unforgiving master which is referred to as The Nature? Humans have been the least endowed as far as the physical attributes are concerned. Lions and tigers have strength, stealth and grace. Elephants have physical might, birds can fly, vipers have venom, panthers can run fastest while horses can run very incredible long distances, the list goes on and on.

But none of these, rules the world! Who rules? You, my friend you! And why? Because you have a brain the seat of intelligence which has found effective ways to overcome the physical minuses. Very pleasing statement! And how much of this organ is used by a common man? In spite of the evolution spread across millions of years you would be surprised that the brain of the great Einstein is preserved, stored and researched. He used just two percent more than what we are supposed to. We use less than five percent of the available potential of the brain in the entire life time.

You would be wondering. Why this build up? The reason is simple. I want to remind you that before you say that you cannot do a thing, please ask yourself a question. Do you have any unused capacity of your brain? Suddenly you would realise that nothing is impossible. May be a bit improbable, but never impossible, when you set your mind on, pursue and persevere with. If you really wish, want something you would do anything and accomplish anything.

I am trying to invite your attention to a basic fact that you and you alone are the most "magical component" of anything you undertake. You may have the best situations, people, equipment, plenty of funds, and yet without you and your involvement you have best chance of failing. Please think. If you are so important so vital, why you have been so casual, so underrated, to such an extent that you almost cease to exist?

Let us come back to the point whether you can sell or not? I believe that every person is a born salesman. Every man is selling something throughout his life. Either he is selling to someone or some one is selling to him. This is a lifelong process, but the funny part is that this comes to us in natural way but not in a professional way. We just do not accept that we can sell.

Right from childhood we use the selling techniques. We promote ourselves for a role in a musical, or a drama, for a class monitorship or many such activities. We are doing everything that a salesman does, but we are not aware. We check for the moods of our parents (before we put forth the demand for a motorcycle), we check up the financial environment of our household, we go out of our normal ways and are on our best behaviour, before we actually initiate our sale. You would agree that we rarely failed. In the language of sales, you closed the deal formally. The kids and salesmen have one thing in common trait. They do not take **no** for an answer.

Once the formal education is over and done with the hardest phase in the life of a young man starts. He prepares his biodata, and sends it to the future employers. Biodata is the best **sales pitch,** he has undertaken. He promotes himself, **by** projecting his qualities, skills and experience. In sales it is called detailing.

He or she definitely sell him or her for a job, promotion, or for a foreign assignment. Don't you do this?

Are you not a born salesman?

But in the course of your career, when you feel that you are settled, you suddenly find that you have lost the knack of selling. And you start to proclaim that you cannot sell. It is funny! The skill which you have so far so successfully used is suddenly gone. You may be educated in any discipline, such as science, commerce, engineering, medicine, law, or fine arts Please rest assured that to reach the top bracket you would have to use your inherent skills of salesmanship. Watch all the top people in any profession they would have the following qualities, either in part or full.

- They dress well
- They know their subject well
- They have a knack of communication
- They have a high level of pleasant persuasion
- They generally do not take no for an answer
- They have a sense of timing
- They are very aware of the changes in environment around them
- They give very good services to their clients.

Now if you notice that the above are the things which a salesman has to do throughout his life. But if you ask any of the above whether he can sell and the answer would be a bug No.

Why this happens? I have tried to rationalise the instant aversion to sales. The selling probably reminds them of the discomfort they had to face in the initial stages of their careers, they want to get away with it. Now they are quite **settled, successful and nothing to do with the below level selling.**

What is the origin of this feeling of discomfort?

1. In the past you were imposing at least you felt so, for your own products or services, now there is no such need.
2. Fear of rejection. In the early stage of your careers, you were rejected many times, but you somehow sustained. There was no ego prestige or social status attached so it did not matter. You knew that the rejection was not personal. It was painful but it was a part of life. To understand that the rejection is more idea oriented takes some time. The pain that comes with rejection is very personal.

3. Fear of failure. When you put the idea, concept or a product you supplement it with your personality, ego and pride so when it fails, it hurts. Does it mean that the fear of failures is only with the beginners? No, it is not so. In fact, the stakes are much more and bigger for the successful people. Sunil Gavaskar, the original little master said that in spite of hundreds by the dozens, after so much success every time he went to open the innings he had the same number of butter flies in his stomach as he had when he made the debut. The anxiety was even more prominent. If this is true then how come the successful people appear so serene, so calm on the outside? Inside they are as afraid as the common beginner, but they have somehow learnt to have a better cover up on their doubts. They have understood that it is a matter of time before the fear fades away. Please understand if are afraid to fail you may never even start in the first place. The importance of failures is to be understood. It is only on the dark backdrop of failures the success shines. Success in isolation, that is, without failure has no meaning. The scale of success is measured on the volume of failures. The humility to accept failures can be the first step of the success, successful people even if they know that they would fail never reduce the levels of efforts. The successful people have learnt the trick of using their past failures as a spring board rather than a hammock. They do not recline and regret. Practice in a perfect way if you want to become perfect or you would be perfect in wrong things. Whatever makes you uncomfortable, **do it until you are a master of the same.** If you are afraid, or conscious of talking to strangers, then just talk to more strangers. It would make a perfect person for a cold call in the future.

4. Fear of a change. When a person is in his thirties, he is more often than not fallen in to a groove. The set routine of life makes him very comfortable. He has adjusted to the limits of earnings and limits of success. He has accepted his lots as his destiny and is at least outwardly happy. He anticipates that because he has so far survived, he would continue to do so. As a matter of fact, he starts calling his life as a **life style. He tries to justify, protect, and defend** his present status and says that it is the best he could have bargained for. But deep down in his mind he knows that he could have been better. Further he knows that he alone is responsible for his present lots, but he rarely acknowledges the fact. He blames his parents, teachers, family but never blames himself. He is in a dark cave and he is in a frustrated state of mind. Everyone knows that if you have to change the way you live you have to change the way you think. Some do change the ways they think and then they change their lots. Steve Jobs is a classic example. He succeeded twice on a scale which is incomprehensible to most of us.

Finally, what creates panic in the minds who say that they cannot sell, who say that selling is not their cup of tea is the basic fact that unlike other professions there is no placc to hide in the sales. You are afraid of the periodical appraisals, reviews where in your performance is ruthlessly analysed. The weekly, monthly, quarterly and annual appraisals can be very painful and exhausting.

But with all these aspects sales can be a very interesting activity and career. It gives you an accelerated exposure and you are generally smarter than the rest of the world. Moreover, if you really think so can you be really away from the sales? Probably no!

So, when you next time say that cannot sell.... take a pause, think for a moment and then only say whatever comes to your mind.

***

CHAPTER THREE

THE MARKET

THE MARKET

The market is the actual field where all your inherent and acquired skills as a marketer and or salesman are duly tested on a day-to-day basis. It can turn out be a battlefield or a walk in a garden depending upon many things. Till today no exact definition of market is actually available, but it is a place that is responsible for commercial transactions beyond any reasonable limits. It encompasses and controls a really huge activity which is throughout the world across the countries, time zones, races, religions, caste, creed and currencies. Over a period of centuries, it has evolved in to a mind-boggling proportion, speed, and volumes. So many different products, so many classes of services, so many industries, so many different salesmen, and so many different customers are daily involved in the *making* or sometimes *breaking* of a viable market.

As a salesman you should know that different products need different expertise and approaches. On the whole, the market can be classified into following:

1. Consumer
2. Consumables
3. Consumer durables

4. Institutional
5. Industrial
6. Trade
7. Cooperative
8. Corporate.
9. Conceptual
10. Space marketing
11. Ethical or pharma sales
12. Government sales
13. Shopping malls.
14. Digital and On-line marketing

May be in the future some more categories would be added but the basic rules would generally be same as they are today. I have tried to analyse the basic needs for dealing in each of the types in this chapter. Once you learn the basic selling you would need to learn specific tricks of the trade. A little bit of fine tuning is needed on a continuous basis, to maximise the benefits as different products would need different approaches.

1. **Consumer**: Consumer market where we get involved on a daily basis as a consumer or as a salesman and of course the shop owners. The category of the product has very little to do on product-to-product basis. This is a fine example of many consumers reaching one place for many products. The individual stakes are comparatively less (as the cost of product is less), but the cumulative impacts can be huge. Does it mean that this particular segment is easy to handle and can be managed with relative ease? No, not at all! The actual time of interaction of the consumer and the salesman is minimal. No sales pitches. The dealer plays an important

role. The point of purchase can be important at as on today. This segment is facing serious challenges from the supermarkets, online sales etc. but so far it has survived in a decent manner. Philip Kotler in one of his predictions had said that the display space and ease of foot fall would decide the survival of retail sales activity. He was right as usual. There is a fierce fight for the space in the shops. The product displays are at premiums. The points of purchase (POP) promotional activities are very cutthroat and strenuous. Earlier the shopkeepers were less demanding, now they have also picked the tricks of the trade. So, they demand their pound of flesh in the trade promotions. All major players like Colgate, Godrej, P&G, HLL, Nirma, Patanjali, Dabur, Nestle, Cadbury, Novino batteries, oils, cosmetics, fight literally for an inch of the display space. In fact, the daily sales reports have a designated section on the display of each outlet. Company like Hindustan Lever has one of the most detailed and comprehensive reports. How much data is generated and how much it is put to improve the lots of the consumer is a point of debate and serious research.

However, the salesman who manages the consumer product ranges should have preferably following profile.

- He should be a fast worker as he has to contact 100 counters per day.
- He should evoke trust and should be well behaved. Mild person is more likely to succeed.
- He may not be very intelligent but must have some basic integrity. He needs a honeybee approach.

- Most of the retailers would tell you that they prefer to see same person representing same company for some length of time. The major complaint is that the salesmen change too soon for their comfort. The lack of trust emerges as the result.

One has to really feel for the persons in consumer sales and appreciate their unending and many times unforgiving grind. It is not at all easy to contact hundred counters on a daily basis for years to come. They do this monotonous routine for almost thirty years, before burning out. The irony is that even after such a vicious grind they rarely know anything very little about actual selling much less about marketing. Even today with all digital warfare the salesman still remains the final link of the entire marketing strategy designed by either a designated brand manager and /or marketing manager. Even today the line sales people are yet to receive the credit due to them. With the mobile tabs and scrutiny, the only human participant is reduced to a mechanical input.

It is of common knowledge that the 4 Bs are the most difficult product ranges to handle. They are Bulbs/ Batteries/ Biscuits and Blades. These are the fastest changing fields and to keep up to the ever-changing requirements of these B's turn out the toughest and the best salesmen in the consumer field.

1. **Consumables**- This category is more or less similar to the earlier consumer except that in here the *same* customers are have to be serviced more often. The same can be also attached to the industrial marketing. It is more dependent on dealers than the consumer.

2. **<u>Consumer Durables</u>**- This category is the so-called glamourous range of products. Televisions, refrigerators, washing machines, air conditioners, coolers, vacuum cleaners, food processors/ mixers, mobiles, together form a "White Goods Category". The atmosphere is very plush, posh, very well-lit and almost jazzy type. Today again this sector is facing the crisis due to digital marketing like Amazon, and others. The dealer here also deals with retails but the difference is in the frequency of buying. The consumer durables are purchased mostly once in a lifetime. If very optimistically put it may be once in ten years. Then what makes this sector tick? The margins used to be very good till in the late eighties of last century. Some companies enjoyed advance bookings, shortages, and even premiums. But it was too good to last. In the beginning of the nineties the slump had started. The tactics changed. The giants like Sony, LG, started their own showrooms. There was a huge boom in the supermarkets. Like Big Bazar, Reliance, and so many others. The retail outlet dealer was suffering very badly. Later the super bazars were put to dust by the online marketing companies like Amazon, Snapdeal. The outlets were reduced by more than half. They either closed or diversified. The only lever or advantages the lonely dealer had been the advantage of providing credit to the customers.

Earlier and the first to enter with the hire purchase schemes was unexpectedly the Citi Bank. It was the reason for the change in the demand equation. Just a few months later State Bank of India followed with a Big Buy scheme. Now every finance company worth its name has a plan or two for all those who want to buy but have no ready cash. The advertisements of *zero percent interest* or "Just pay 100 and take home a TV/Washing Machine/ even a car." Type ads are abundant in the trade. This is one of the major reasons because of which this consumer durable trade is flourishing. It is surprising to see the manufacturers like Bajaj have their own finance company. It is a miracle of the last decade. The banks and the finance companies promote their schemes with such a heavy hand that most gullible customers feel that they are getting the product almost as a gift. Sadly, this is too big a game with even bigger rackets. The salesman in this category has to be sincere towards the company he works for or else his days are numbered. He has to be smart, clear headed, and pretty fair towards the products, dealers and the customers. If this equilibrium is not achieved, it would result in a threat to his existence. The dealers are more powerful, they have a hotline to the top brass of the company and hence they can overpower the salesperson with ease. Considering all odds, it can be safely said that the duty of the salesman in the white goods category is to **convert the pull** created by heavy advertisements in to **actual conversion** in to revenue at the retail counter. if he fails the entire campaign and promo schemes would be utterly wasted.

The salesman in this area have evolved into extra smooth variety which is quite irritating most of the times. But that is how it is.

4) <u>**Institutional**</u>: Institutional sales can be termed as an off shoot of the hire and purchase schemes. The basic advantage is bulk purchase at a single point. Moreover, you have already taken care of the competition. You have as clear a field as you can ever wish to have. This is a very specialised job and needs various skills like, sustained

relationship building, extra attention to services offered and continuous follow up. You have to be aware that your competitors are also on the prowl to spoil your party. The span of time from the initiation of the enquiry to the actual placement of the order and further smooth execution may be six months or even more. So before starting the process the salesman must check that the person, the decision maker would be around for at least one year. There are so many examples where a near complete deal fall apart because of the transfers or even the retirements of the dealing authority. The absolute pain of reporting the deal going bust. All the efforts of earlier six months, and high sales projections fall flat and your management would be mad at you. The ridicule is too heavy. The second thing to be primarily checked is the financial condition of the prospect. If it is a government department or undertaking then the policy must remain at least for one year. The third and probably the most important thing is how closely you can handle the deal. Or else you would do all the hard work, toil for months and end up in getting nothing. Some smarter competitor would jump in with lesser prices and just snatch the deal. The only things that change in the order is the name of the product and the lower price. The officers have a readymade offer with proper justification and even approvals. The fewer persons know about your deal is the only security you have. The other people from the department also have their axes to grind. They also have their contacts. And never forget you own colleagues they can backstab at the first chance. So, be very careful and then you may be really enjoying the fruits of success.

5. **Industrial**: The industrial sector is the hardest or the easiest selling area depending upon what types of industries you are supposed to contact. Let us see the

harder part first.

The customer here is sharp. Most likely he is more intelligent and more experienced. He is more qualified and he may be an expert in the field say manufacturing or maintenance. He sees no point in dealing with incompetent salesman. He is already overstressed. And hence he may have very little tolerance levels. Actually, there is no reason for anyone to tolerate a salesman's stupidity. Trying to *convince* such a tough professional is a waste of time. If you try the age-old approach of "Our product is the best, cheapest, etc.... etc" you have lost the match without a ball being bowled. Here he is doing what he knows best for the last ten years and suddenly a most unlikely person in the form of the salesman trying to tell him that he would do better if he follows the salesman.

To deal with these you have to be thorough, in your product knowledge, technology used, and its practical and actual application in the process used by them. In industry what sells is the correct demo of the product than the sales pitch. What he sees he does either agree or does not. Talking has to be replaced by doing.

One more difficult part in the industrial sales is the limited number of customers. You have to establish yourself first then your products. Moreover, these days the industries barring a few are in a mess, they are what is known as hand to mouth. Hence the salesman has to be very clear about the credit terms, delivery schedules and payment terms.

After all the difficulties, the *easy part* comes from the fact that they know exactly what they want. Product wise and pricewise it is a race between you and the competition. One more easy thing is what was the hard part initially. You must recall the time you had to spend to make the industrial customer for shifting from his conventional to your type of products. So, you can be assured that unless your product quality dips you have a steady flow of orders. Salesman has to know the concept of down time in the industry and should take care that his products or their shortage is not the reason for the downtime. When you have an established channel, it becomes easy for you introduce new ranges and improved versions of existing products. Industrial selling is a difficult, demanding exercise but it is also gratifying because it deals in huge numbers and revenue.

6.Trade: The trade market is all inclusive term and probably teaches maximum to the aspiring sales and marketing professional. Trade market is mainly a combination of stockists, dealers, sales partners, and all such facilities which are

Included in the activity called trade. The trading term has different meaning when referred to in the context of the shares and stock market.

TRADE MARKET

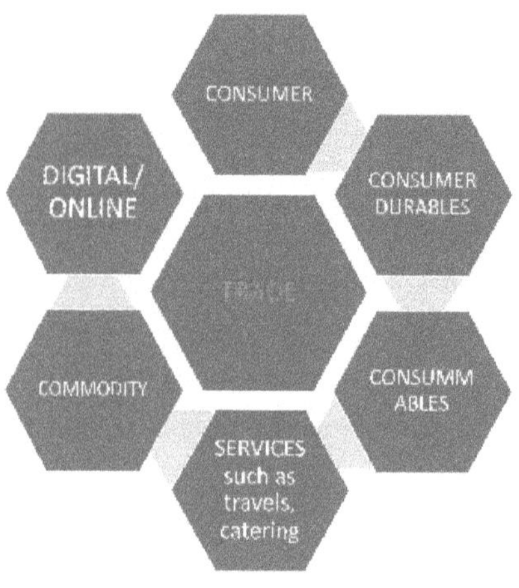

Typical Trade Market

Dealers is a special category and part of the society. The role of dealer gets defined and reviewed in every society depending upon the lifestyle of the particular society. The complicated relationship between the dealer and the producer of the goods is very difficult to understand and operate. There is trust or lack of it, there is a feeling of association or a fight for the share of the profit, the see saw is very interesting. The salesman who understands the dealers and their role in the overall development of the company generally finds a balance and leads a comfortable life. If trade business is properly handled it can be very beneficial for the manufacturer. The criteria on which the dealership is finalised can be the key to the later success. It should be rational and process based rather than based on caste, community, region, religion or even language.

These days some new terms are used. They are as follows.

SPA- Sales Promotion Agents

DCA- Dealer cum Applicator

Partners in Trade

Some more would be coming as the pattern of the sales and distribution would change. Again, Indians have shown an unnecessary hurry in adopting the American pattern over their traditional ways which helped them to rule the world for thousands of years.

Coming back to our salesman. He must remember one primary thing to avoid future complications. "That he is *paid by the company* he works for and that the company would keep doing so long as the dealers perform as per the norms of the company. The thin line always exists between the manufacturer and the dealers which must be maintained. It is comparable to the relationship in the family like the real brothers and cousins. The trade market actually teaches the salesman much more than he could ever learn by way of training in the company. Each dealer is a different, separate pulsating *entity* and presents exclusive and customised set of advantages and problems. Hence each is special!

7. Co-operative sector: This sector is a relatively new wing of sales activity. It started somewhere in early sixties. It is very peculiar to the Indian politics and the political leadership *generally rules and exploits* this sector. It is one of the darkest examples of power misuse and personal agenda. However, gladly there are happy exceptions in Amul, Lijjat. Coming back to our salesman! He would be dealing with cooperative businesses if he is selling seeds, fertilisers, pump sets, irrigation systems, pesticides, or the school accessories as well as the items dealt by the social welfare ministry. The purchases are in huge quantities and hence a lot is at stake. Generally, the purchase is made by the society which can be either consumer society or consumer credit society. The society can be the primary model for the trade in rural market. If your products are of the rural type, you must learn all aspects of cooperative trade. The president, the secretary and in some cases the technical officer form the decision-making unit. With the advent of easy finance schemes this channel enjoys the exclusive attention and can be very effective if properly used.

8. Corporate: When the marketing is done at the corporate management level it can be called as the corporate marketing. One example may explain.

The story goes like this: A very big multinational organization having its corporate office in Mumbai, was negotiating an extraordinary deal in Bangalore. It was in crores of rupees. The direct demand officer, (DDO) was of the level of a Deputy Chief Engineer in the concerned government department. The order was delayed and was almost lost because the Bangalore office of the company could not generate enough force. Incidentally, the Chairman of the company was in Bangalore. He was being briefed by the concerned regional manager. The on-the-spot feedback on the status of the almost lost order, was too much for the firebrand new generation Chairman. He could not accept and hence visited the office of the DCE. He went unannounced. The Chairman sent his visiting card. The DCE was out of his wits and came running out of his office, greeted the Chairman, and was waiting for any clue for the visit. The DCE was very aware that the Chairman was held in very high esteem by the department bosses, including the Minister. The Chairman was a smart person. He talked about everything except his own company. When enough steam was created to cook everything up, the Chairman got up to leave and wished the best to the DCE. And just when he was leaving, he as a parting remark he informed the DCE that his Bangalore office was talking about some order that was held up. Further he said that if there was anything he could do for the same.

Can you guess what happened afterwards? Next week the order was received by at Bangalore Regional Office. This time around the regional manager was out of his wits, because he never knew that the Chairman had visited the DCE out of turn. His suspense ended when the marketing manager told him the story during their monthly meeting at Mumbai.

Please note that such a thing happens once in a decade.

<u>9.Conceptual</u>- One more term that is the gift of the late nineties which earned quite a reputation is the conceptual selling/ marketing. After the so-called opening of the market in the futuristic conditions there was either a great influx of foreign ideas, concepts and product lines. There was appointed reference to anything that was Indian and it was promoted that whatever was western was better. After the outbreak of many endemics and pandemics the bubble has finally burst. But in those days, it was very fashionable to call the products as conceptual etc. The concepts like cosmetics, wellness products, linen, cotton, minimum acccss surgeries, epoxy materials, high quality non-stick coatings, vacuum cleaners, smps, ultra sound and MRI imaging are some of the few one can recall. Some were really very stunning while others were not so. But these ranges created a sales force which was very similar to the missionaries. They were talking of things ahead of the present time to the people who were pretty rigid. The secret of the success was in the skill with which you

dispersed the new knowledge without ever creating a single bit of antagonism. The basic thing was *not to say* anything negative about the present and conventional methods or equipment. The salesman had to acknowledge right in the beginning about the services so far given by the traditional methods. This simple approach made the customer to feel smart and good about himself. NOW, if the customer has to continue being smart and further updated then should just listen to what the salesman had to say. He would adopt the new products because he wants to. That too for the betterment of his own activity and earn more revenue and respect.

The concept marketers were helped beyond any reasonable limits by the people who were in the top tier of the society. The concept of utility, and economy was slowly replaced by in step with the western world. And supposedly equal to them. The concept marketers almost always concentrated on the younger generations.

10. Space Marketing- When a person is comfortable with twenty-four hours deadlines or even less, he should think of going in the field of space marketing. In common language it means collecting advertisements for the daily newspapers, magazines and other print media. Please note it is one of the most interesting and toughest fields to work in. You are tested on a daily basis that too on a straight forward centimetre by centimetre. The competition activity is also very visible. In fact, the daily meeting of the press can be very pleasant or very explosive. The customer is given a brief based on the readership, ad recall, cost per view and many such things. It is very flashy and unpredictable market. The figures are generally cooked up, if not manipulated.

a) Print Media: In space marketing the basic tools are the ABC (Audit Bureau of Circulation) NRS (National Readership Survey) and a few others. The agencies involved are National Readership Survey Council, INS (Indian News Society), AAAI (Advertising Associations of India) and the ABC. Despite of the big names the data still needs to be discounted and evaluated by different standards. Again, the relationship between the circulation and the readership has never been analysed in a way it should be. Maybe, it is because the publications are run by the politicians who are rarely interested in the truth. As a media manager one has to learn the relationship of the newsprint consumption, and the actual figure of circulation. We are very smart and have an ability to exploit any possible loopholes in any system. What baffles any sensible person is the incorrect circulation figures?

One of my media manager friends told me that the discount factor is about thirty percent less than the reported figures. Secondly the analysis of demography of the readership is very peculiar to say the least. The sample size of the survey is very rarely reported correctly. So even after the data, its analysis, and smooth language of the space selling person the media managers depend upon the age-old system. So, the smart marketing people who design the media campaigns generally go by the response to the *actual response coupons and /or mail box responses rather* than the circulation, readership, and ABC analysis.

As reader of any newspaper, you can find by your own interest in any advertisements you see daily. The time spent on reading the newspaper is generally in minutes. Project your figures and you would have a fair idea about the efficacy of the advertisements. Economic Times generally carries the updated versions of the NRS as well as the TRP figures. They help as a light house.

When every newspaper or publication claims number one in one or the other category. To test these claims is very essential for the correct efficacy of the media management. Media test marketing is a must or your money just would evaporate very fast.

But as earlier said space marketing is a very challenging field. In all other fields the deadline is on a monthly basis. In print media it is twenty-four hours. What is printed today has no relevance tomorrow. Very few in sales can cope with this relentless pressure of performing. Add to this a boss who knows what he should know and then you may not have a single day of happiness. But if you are working for a decent publication and performing well as per the expectations of your boss space marketing is the best field to work in.

b) Audio Visual media: What can one really say about this very jazzy, fast, ruthless, and flashy field? When people say AV media as the ultimate monster created in the 20th century I tend to agree. The lack of quality, the coarse clothes or lack of them, the mindless promotion of mediocrity, the frequency of advertisements, is really beyond any comprehensions. They have TRP very similar to the ABC etc.

What business are they really in? They are in the business of revenue generation, nothing else. Rest whatever they do, is the classical moh maya as in the Hindu philosophy. They make us watch the advertisements whether we want to or not. In the earlier days of television and NET we could at least switch the channels off or start surfing for the channels. They are smart and they have now synchronised the advertisements so even if you search for other channels you end up watching something you never want to buy. Their ill effect on the sub conscious minds is visible. I am really worried for the next generations. They must have a heart of steel to escape from the effects of monstrous hammering of the advertisement's day in and day out. Once in a while you may see a good commercial but that is an exception. The relationship between the concept of the ad and the products is microscopic to say the least. Many times, you remember the ads but not the product and vice versa. What we see on the screen is quite disgusting but what we hear about the backstage activities of the ad agencies, models, their life styles are devastating. Why we have to see the ads of condom, sanitary napkins, energy capsules, on the family shows? Are they I really needed? We are moving away from the ethos, traditions, culture of our great nation and sadly no body is bothered. I feel that the Indians are masters in giving up things. No other country, no other community has given up so much of their own culture and adopted trash from outside. You can list at least thousand things which we have left.

But again, who are we to change what is happening? The AV field is a specialised field. The person here has to be a visionary to predict the future of any ad campaign. Whatever little I have seen of this huge industry makes me shudder. Only thing I can say this field requires a particular type to succeed if you are a little loud, extra smooth, very good in languages, very flexible about working hours, late nights, party animal, then and then only you should think of entering this razzle dazzle of a field. What we are talking is only for the marketing aspect.

11. Ethical (Pharmaceutical)markets: One of the most glamourised markets in the last century is now on the verge of losing all its sheen. The ethical part is diminishing very fast. The cuts, the commissions, the tax evasions, the foreign trips, the unnecessary prescriptions, are some of the things which can be reviewed.

Earlier it used to be a huge market which used to cater hundreds of millions of people on a daily basis. The people who worked here were smartly dressed, and had earned a respect from the field. In fact, in the early seventies any person wearing a neck tie was automatically associated with pharma sales. The term was M.R. As a student of sales and marketing I am always fascinated by these people and their activity. Also, I have healthy respect for these types. If we have to use the current term *of bio bubble* then these people have their own variety of different if not distinguished business bubble. The ethical detailing as they call it is easy and difficult. They deal with one of the most hyped and qualified community of the society *the doctors*. To talk to, to motivate the doctor to prescribe the medicines manufactured by your company is no mean feat. Everyone in India knows about the majority of the problems in the medical and pharma field. Many of my friends are working in pharma field have narrated experiences about the "noble" profession. In the recent extra ordinary pandemic situation stories from medical field were shocking and fascinating. We are not discussing the *what should be done aspect* so I would come back to pharma selling. No profession is independent of the society and medicine sadly is no exception.

The MR as he is called is now a term just like a manager. There is no gender bias. Many ladies have chosen pharma selling as their career and they are performing admirably. Ladies probably have an inherent talent for counselling and convincing and that is very visible in the activity. Very surprisingly, even if the MR is one of the most visible persons, he rarely sees his actual customer. The process of pharma selling is very typical. A company manufactures or formulates as it is referred to some medicines, its designated MR details the products to the doctors, then doctor prescribes some of the products to the patients and some retailers then actually sell these products to the consumers. So simple, is it? And throughout the process the MR is responsible for the effective movement of the products. It is one of the most coordinated processes as each component rarely sees the other and depends fully on his participation.

How difficult it must be to estimate the demand of a particular drug, then to ensure the proper detailing to the prescribing doctors, then ensuring that the appropriate area retailers maintain the required stocks for the selling. The entire process is simply astonishing and that it continues is almost a miracle, as there is no contact with the actual consumer at the cash conversion point of purchase. For the companies with some reputation like Glaxo, Cipla, Abbot, Torrent, Cadilla, and many others it may be relatively easy. But can you spare a thought for a MR of say a company called "Ganga Mata Pharma". What must be his pitch, how he must be creatin demand, and later fulfil it? It is simply amazing!

These days many negative aspects are attached to pharma selling but they are not as rule. So even today the old routine of pharma selling is followed.

Yes, the pharma companies used to have the best training facilities in our country. The results were bearing it out. Companies like Ciba, Pfizer had a long induction and then on the job training programs. There was a visible difference in a person. He came out almost as a new version. Now in spite of the glow and shine or the money involved the pharma sales people are under tremendous pressure and generally look tense. The relaxed approach is gone. The pressure of targets is very visible. What ails this once very promising industry is very complex and needs a detailed review and analysis. Is it because medical profession is a pale shadow of it earlier noble version? Or is it because the unethical promotion? Or is it because the mediocrity of the doctors or the MRs? Is it the combination of pharma and insurance which is killing the nobility?

The sales person in other fields must take heart from these pharma sales people and do their jobs with more interest and determination for the simple and one reason that they can at least see their customers.

12.The Government: It is one of the largest buyers of anything under the blue. It is a wonderland like field and those like Alice have only a free access to the same. This market is generally not open for lesser mortals like us. There are authorised and unauthorised agents. Sadly, the second version is more prominent even today. Most of the funds were and are spent over those products which the government may never need. Why? Because some nephew or son in law of some minister may have the agency for this range of products. Millions of rupees are still wasted. May be this is the area which is the road to the sudden affluence of some politically connected people in India. You may recall hundred stories of rags to riches stories in your area. Multiply them for each such area and you may have the idea about the extent of the loot and corruption. Again, this is not the scope of this essay. But sales can never be discussed in isolation.

There are many reasons and many processes which are used, manipulated and twisted to suit the requirement of pleasing the ministers. The employees are bound by the rules and precedents. They are experts in reducing the pace and efficiency of the process. Everything on paper is done correctly, following all rules laid down by the people probably living in the caves. The people even from Mughal era would have found the rules of government *out of date.*

But in spite of all these *stringent* rules there are many examples of matchboxes sold for hundred rupees each, a pen for twenty rupees, when these things are available for one rupee per piece. Why this happens? Because nobody from top to bottom is interested in anything except his own percentage from the deal. Tremendous intentional inertia, corruption, favouritism, nepotism, under hand dealings are the major features of this huge irresponsibly handled sector. The irony further is that all people here are qualified and technically competent, but they lack simple integrity. The quality control in government sector is a big joke. Whether it is simple mid-day meals for the deprived or *the software* for the income tax department of central government. The cases of corruptions are never solved because the judiciary is also of questionable integrity.

<u>Just one example:</u>

In the recent past a state electricity board has levied a new levy on the hapless consumers. It is called transmission losses. This is a case of utter shamelessness. Let us see why?

The state electricity boards called as SEBs have the one of the largest pools of technical competence in form of the engineers. Some body technically qualified in the SEB specified the sizes of the conductors, or transmission lines. They were of course within the acceptable tolerance levels. Somebody more experienced than the middle level engineer must have approved the specifications and the cost. Some body very senior in the materials then procured the lines. So far so good. No auditor can do anything.

Now suddenly the transmission lines have started to incur more transmission losses. Why?

Who bears the brunt? Of course, the consumer! What happens to all those qualified technically competent people? Nothing! They are enjoying the commissions! The consumer suffers because the states have monopoly. That is one more very peculiar aspect. How all monopoly sectors in government like public transport, railways, steel, cement, power, aluminium, and even gold are making huge losses? It is really comical that people like HP, IOL, SAIL, CIL need a fleet of marketing staff. They may at the most the distribution managers but marketing: a big joke!

Any way, if a salesman chooses to sell in government department, he must have following skills.

- He must be very good in percentages.
- He must develop a thick skin
- No inklings about quality, and about misuse of public money.
- A benign attitude towards corruption
- Additionally, he must have expertise in wines and liquors.

Any person who has dealt with government selling would tell you the government somehow works is a miracle. One expert said that after he had a stint in government sales he started believing in God.

He should also have a clear idea about all purchase procedures, like DGS&D, CSPO, CSD, RATE Contracts, tenders and their types, digital tendering, digital signatures, and all topical new things that enter the department. One small bit of relevant information is worth in millions of rupees. He should be aware of 3 quotations, 5/3/2 percentages, and its distribution, measurement book (MB) and every small trick of this amazing trade.

***

13. The shopping malls/ super markets: The shopping malls were introduced to Indians in the last decade of last century. The top of the recall is the Big Bazar, or Reliance Super Fresh, and many such who had a great time and now are not seen. Estimated by the Statista.com the estimated number in India is a staggering 12.8 million which includes the traditional variety. The number of customers in the segment is so huge that the top brands in the world are drooling over the prospects of the entry in this segment. There are many socio economic, and demographic issues which would be emerging from this type of markets. Classically the markets developed in the following sequence. A salesman went to customers, then customer started visiting a shop, then many shops in the same area formed the markets, development of wholesale and retails, home delivery types, and even today the interchange is going on. The supermarkets tried to combine many of these features in the projects.

However, the concept of supermarkets is still not very popular in Indian markets. They have become a success in the metro and the minimetro cities. But the traditional market is still surviving is a good thing. The initial benefits offered by the supermarkets are temporary and then the fleecing of the customers starts. Moreover, Indian consumer laws are lax and they do not offer any worthwhile protection to the consumer. The goods return policy, the quality checks, the ambiance, do not match with the international regulations and if they do the implementation is pathetic.

The younger generation is more likely to adopt the culture of supermarkets and malls. The concept of spending a day at the mall is more appealing to them. Buying, eating outside, entertainment by way multiplexes, and even dining at the same place is alluring only to them. The plush atmosphere actually repels the traditional customers. They are wise to know that ultimately every comfort comes out of their pockets.

Coming back to sales aspect one has to concede that these mega stores have changed the concepts of buying. So, almost companies have separate sales force and policies which cater to the megastores. The rates are different, very low as compared to normal wholesalers. The selling in bulk is a special skill and the salesman who have it can be very happy selling to the malls. Again, the supplier has a very little say in the management or display of goods. Everything is chargeable, each inch of the space is severely fought for. The competition is very cutthroat. The quantities are mindboggling, but it is a twenty-four-seven job. If the entry of companies like Costco, Walmart, is seen in the near future then the market of the traditional retail is in deep trouble. The small trader can never compete with these company setups. The old law of big fish eats small fish is very much applicable. The customer has to find what suits him.

For a salesperson this can be like the institutional sales.

14 Digital/ Online/ Web markets: The latest to enter the madness called selling is the digital market. The models developed by Amazon, Snapdeal, Alibaba, has simply zapped the world. No wonder that amazon is in the top three of the world ranking. It is a beautiful concept which does not need any traditional set up. They do not need shops, malls, godowns, and even then, they have captured a major share of the global market. They have no limits for products, production schedules, no labour unions, no area restriction, no language bars, no maps and hence a simple product can reach the globe. The phenomenal success is due to the great vision of the founders.

Coming back to sales aspect, a significant change is there. The change is in the contact mechanism. The entire aspect of *attention* in the classical AIDA model is taken care of by the company software people. The sales people are involved in the vendor development rather than the customer development. This activity is still running on only a few of its million legs. It has already sent ripples in the traditional markets.

Salesman in this area has to be very close to the ground, very able to communicate at least in India with very suspicious small-time artisans, and sometimes cottage industry. In the recent past even the automobile market has shifted to the online version. The key words here are B2B, niche, auction market places, crowdfunding, pocket friendly, MVP, SaaS, and many more. This is a very fast and happening market and things change in an instant. The salesman has to be tech savvy, friendly and a trouble shooter type.

I think we have covered almost all categories of markets, however they keep on merging or separating depending upon place, population, products, prices and other famous Ps of marketing.

***

CHAPTER FOUR

YOU & MARKET

You and Market

By now we have seen what you are and what are the likely places called the market are. They are also called as the **"Field"**, a wise person would read it more like a **battlefield**. Selling is an interaction between the seller and the buyer. Generally, it is heavily loaded in the favour of the buyer at least in the present days.

Let us see the complete process of selling and then marketing before we traverse in the details and intricacies. Selling is one-time activity and when the payment is received the cycle is complete. When the concerted efforts are put in a specific way to ensure that this simple process is repeated again and again between the:

- same product and same buyer
- same product and different buyers,
- different products same buyer
- different products different buyers
- one-time buyers and the repeat buyers
- same area same products
- same area different products

and many such variable combinations it gives a way to one of the complex processes called as marketing of which sales is the integral part. Whatever marketing team does it necessarily has to produce and increase the quantum of sales. These days there is a conscious effort to disassociate from sales. Marketing people do not talk of sales as if it is a job of lesser competence. The most illogical thing to say. Maybe, they are not comfortable about the straight forward and immediately verifiable process of sales.

Many times, many people use sales and marketing as same or equivalent or interchangeable, you have to clearly understand that they are not so. Yes, they are interdependent.

Sales is an effective interaction between a need of a consumer and supply by the seller. We have to ensure that:

- We know how to *find* what one *needs*
- How to fulfil his *specific* need
- How to *ensure* that he gets what he wants or needs

<u>AND</u>

- How to get *equal and fair exchange* for satisfying his needs, by way of money.

Ideally, things should happen in a slow, deliberate and soft initiation way. But in our scenario, a salesman on his first day is given a pep talk about how his products (he is supposed to sell from today or tomorrow) are the best and the company which is of course *better than the best*. If he is lucky, he may get a semblance of the product training from a person, who is distinctly uninterested, which shows in a profound way. The approach of many companies towards the incoming salesman is questionable. The *trainer* is convinced that the incoming person is a passing incident so the seriousness is in proportion to the same. Unfortunately, he even mentions the fact to the incoming salesman.

Next day the incumbent is a "Trained Salesman"!

This book is for such persons and it is hoped that they would feel a little more secure after they read this book.

The actual process of the sales is the classical AIDA model, which includes Attention (Awareness), Interest, Desire and Action. AIDA was first developed by E. St. Elmo Lewis as early as 1910. The same can be applied to all categories of products and consumers. Now of this is true why some are better than others? Why when some go, they always get orders? Why then some people are more composed and confident? As Shiv Khera puts it do they do *different things* or do they *do same things differently*.

The differences are working even before the enquiry is generated.

Basic preparation of the salesman: Apart from what is discussed in the chapter You there are some things the salesman has to know.

1. The salesman **must** have a thorough knowledge about his products. This is absolutely **non-negotiable**. The knowledge comes from the trainings, product literature of your company as well as the competition, further reading some relevant books. The practical input of the problems faced and how they were resolved comes from your dealers as well as form the competition.

   There is a simple test of this process. The knowledge should be such that whenever the problem is mentioned you should instantly recall the relevant product from your range and its advantage over the nearest product from competition. When you can assert that your product can be a better choice without being hypercritical about the products from competition. Please always remember that we are living in an open ended and handed technology world. You would even find that the products are more or less similar. So, you have to establish the pedigree of your products and their efficacy. Avoid best, cheapest, number one, ways of convincing. Ideally you should be in a state of a "casual" dominance, because of your knowledge. All salesmen worth their salt, sadly know that they spend **less** time to improve their lots before the ball is rolled than the time they spend on the subsequent collection and correction of facts reports.

It helps the salesman to check up his bag. The bag of a salesman is sometimes even more important than anything in his life. His bag must be a complete office in itself. (A check list is given in the appendix.) The bag should have from stapler pins to revenue stamps. More time spent here reduces the pain, agony and dejection at a later stage.

The process of sales is depicted in the figure titled as "the retention of interest", there are three basic steps called as *pre-contact, contact and the post-contact*. We would study

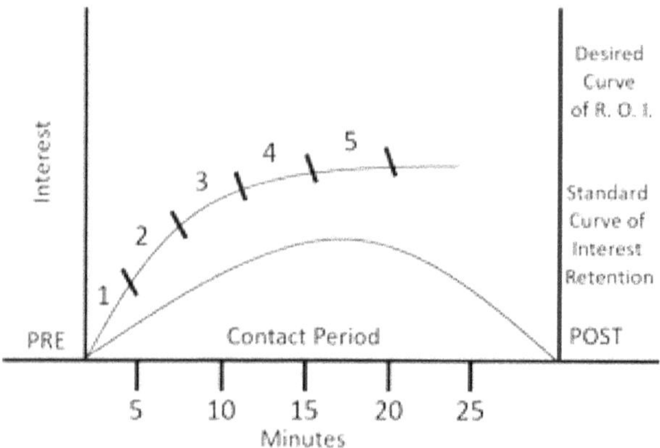

Sales Call

Pre-contact: This is usually a phase of preparation. The better you are here better are the chances of the success. Please collect as much information about your customer you are about to contact.

In case of an industry, you should find out

- The year of the initiation
- Last year's performance
- Percentage of dividend given in the last year
- Any other factory or unit apart from the one you are visiting.
- Is the other unit is already buying your products?
- The frequency and the quantity and the rates offered
- If yes

- ◦ How much and how
- ◦ Do you have order copies?
- ◦ Do you have performance certificates?

- ◦ Are you sure that there were no issues or hassles?

<u>The actual user-</u>

- What type of a person he is?
- Is he a stickler for quality?
- Does he assert himself?
- Is he a good listener?
- Does he have the decision power to place the orders?

<u>In case of a dealer-</u>

- How long is he in the trade?
- How long your company's association with him?
- What is his outstanding payments position?
- Does he promote your products?
- Does he behave with you with respect or he just tolerates your company?
- Does he take pride in the association with you?

In case of a customer (non-Categorised)

- Does he know what he wants?
- Does he have enough money?
- Does he show any specific brand preference?
- Does he believe in listening to you?
- Is he accompanied by his family?
- What category of ABC he belongs to? A or B or C

What you must have observed so far is that a basic guideline is offered to you for you. It is never enough. The complexity keeps on going up or down depending upon your preparations.

Contact: Contacting a customer is the first outside your comfort area task you would be doing. Just like all knowledge outside the swimming pool is useless once you dive in a pool, you would feel very tense nervous and useless. If you would feel so you are a normal human being.

The contact phase is ideally divided into following:

1. Initiation
2. Interest
3. Problem
4. Solution
5. Commercial closing

The process of sales is tested and rated here in this phase. Before we actually study this one must remember that sales call is a professional meeting. He is there for a purpose. **Never ever dilute this focus.**

You should also know that the best sound any man likes to listen to is _his own._ Remember this absolutely clearly. Do not over shadow with your personality aura, smartness, and so-called product knowledge. The inside fact about sales is that the _not so smart,_ and _needy looking_ person is more likely to succeed than the smart and snobbish.

The total time of this process should be usually twenty to twenty-five minutes, unless you are in for a discussion, justification or projects specifications.

1. **Initiation**: This step should never take more than two minutes. The simple purpose is to introduce yourself

and talk about any reference if you have. Do not start parroted speeches. Wait and listen. Listen to even the silence. Silence can be a great help to realise the ambience. The décor of the room, the AC temperature, the face of a person can be your friends.

Apart from a simple introduction the more important purpose is to establish yourself as someone worthwhile to talk to.

Introduction:

a. Please learn to introduce yourself in a neat and succinct way. Ideally you should have three or four scripted variations of how you introduce yourself.
b. Please rehearse in front of a mirror.
c. If possible, get this activity supervised and corrected by your immediate superior.

Please remember that you are supposed to know yourself the best. Can anyone else introduce you in a better way than you. No never! I have seen many sales persons who fumble even while telling their names. That is the worst thing you can do to yourself. It creates an absolute poor first impression. Nothing in a sales function is casual. It is directed towards the next step. So, the basic function of the introduction is to create that little bit of curiosity and readiness to listen to what you would have to say. The potential buyer should think "Oh! Seems to be a good guy! Let me listen to him and what he has to offer."

1. **Interest:** The second most important thing is the arousal of interest of the customer in you and your products. So, try to talk to him about himself. Make him talk about

what interests him. The most likely item would be his recent success. Ask him a very safe question "How does he do what he does? And still look so cool?" Once he starts talking about him and his achievements as well as his work, he feels that he is in control and he feels good. He feels like talking to you. Next you lead him to talk about his problems if any. If he has how does he get rid of them. Does he have any chronic or persistent problems? Make him talk about his problems. He would give a load of relevant and not so relevant information. Listen to him very carefully, and ask your mind to channelise this flow and come out with the plausible solutions.

2. **Problem:** When the customer shows you his problems and wounds never shirk away. His problems are yours if you want to sell. Be interested in his problems even if you know that _you do not have products_ to cater to his needs. _Please listen very carefully_. Try to sympathise with him, but never overreact. Whatever you do please do not create an impression that you are superior to the person in front of you.

Next on a piece of a paper do following exercise.

- Identify the problem as exactly as possible.
- Get is confirmed by the customer
- Decide the limits and tolerances acceptable to the customer.
- Please be clear that you give solutions to a specific, clear and predefined problem. Otherwise, you would find that after you give the solution, the size of the problem grows, just like the nose of Pinocchio.

4. **Solution:** Providing solutions to the problems posed by the customer forms the most important part apart from concluding the deal. This decides the quality of your relationship between you, and your *would be* and even *existing* clients. However, in both the cases the changes or differences are pretty minor. Before you provide a solution to a specific problem you should have done a simple exercise.

ABC LIMITED
Mr. Anand Gupte
NOIDA
22/08/ 2020

Sr.No.	Problem posed	Solutions with options
1		
2		
3		
4		

Sales is Ideally Solving Problems

The sheet should have the name of the company, person of contact, date and place.

One more rule is followed. Never offer solutions in a dictatorial way. At the same time do not appear condescending. Do not for your own sake appear smarter than the client even if you think so. Do not be over bearing.

Try to offer solutions with options. Explain the cost benefits of each option. To be able to choose maintains his ego. Once the options are given stop for a moment. Let the person analyse his own situation in the light of the most likely solution. Let that computer of work inside and wait for a printout.

Once the solutions are mentally accepted quite a few things would happen. The most important from your point of view is that you would be a part of the team, along with, your customer which may have to work together for the necessary approvals and /or sanctions. You are a team and imagine with whom, "Your Customer"! What better deal can you ask for?

<u>5.Commercial Closing:</u> Closing is the last lap of the race. You have run nicely. But even in the actual race if you do not run the last lap properly you lose the race. Same here! The proper closing alone decides whether or not you are profitable.

By now you must be ready with a mental offer to be presented to the customer. It always helps writing the offer in the presence of the customer. Make a best offer as a quotation and wait. The customer is on the threshold of the decision which needs backing up by finance. Till now he was happy that he was getting solutions for his problems. Now the <u>scene</u> changes, and he has to think of provision of funds. He may have to take necessary sanctions. If possible, please insist and somehow meet the decision-making person with him. This single step cuts down a lot of time lag and delays. Once the approval is obtained, please insist for an order. If immediate order is not possible at least get a letter of intent.

One last tip!

After you get the order just say good bye and leave the scene as early as possible. Thank them and leave.

By now, are you thinking the different ways you have been handling the process. Did you get any fresh ideas? Please understand that you have to be different if not distinguished from all other salesmen who have parroted their way out of the minds of the customers. You have proved that you are friend, as solution provider, rather than a mere salesman.

<u>Post contact:</u> Once your precontact and contact periods are over, you have to ensure your commitments regarding prices, delivery schedules, and after sales services. The reason is if you somehow keep the right profile, you have developed a contact and you can spare that extra time on some other customer or products. It should be simple but sadly it is not. The details are discussed in the chapter called "the internal selling".

Every salesman who wants to excel in the sales field, should do this post contact activity very seriously. Have checks on what produces best results and then just repeat the process. You would know that you have achieved the level of skills required, by the increase in orders and less of outstanding payments. And if you are lucky even by a promotion.

CHAPTER FIVE

THE PURCHASE MANAGERS

<u>THE PURCHASE MANAGERS</u>

As the other side of the coin, you would meet a variety of purchase managers. I also have. They are very typical. They deserve a respect for the simple reason that they allow you to talk, present your products despite of their crack schedules.

Imagine you are a purchase manager, and mentally occupy his chair. Daily, you would be facing a battery of salesmen; some smart others not so smart. On a daily basis. Imagine also listening to following about one hundred times a day, in person or on telephone.

"Sir, my product is the best, the cheapest, and most suitable for your needs. Our services are world class. But you would never need them. Just give us one chance and you would live happily ever after." Just read this for ten times.

Do you realise the pain? Do you feel the pain?

For the sheer torture at the hands of the salesmen I respect these people. I was told that these days the personal encounters are somewhat replaced by emails, and video calls. It must be a great relief. During my interactions with the purchase managers, I came to know some very humorous and some very humiliating stories. Their number is so large that a separate book might be needed.

The purchase manager has to be smart and alert. If he falters a bit and the production is held up, he may receive the classical kick in the butt. The PM faces a double-edged sword all the time. The management theories about the stocks maintaining, the economic order quantity (EOQ), First In First Out (FIFO), or Last In First Out (LIFO), payment terms, credit control, and many such terms can make him as uncomfortable as a cat on a hot roof. How many times we see a desperate PM running from pillar to post to meet the erratic production demands. The assembly line is very threatening. The deadlines are really lethal. Most material is needed on yesterday basis. The planning and all such things are more talked about than followed.

The second factor which is checked by the management is the credit. If anything is bought on cash, it arises quite a few eyebrows. What follows is the scrutiny of the situation and circumstances which prompted such an emergency cash purchase. It is what is the HR calls as a black spot.

The third factor which is under the microscope is the compliance of after sales services by the vendors. It requires a great coordination and it turns out as a thankless job for the PM.

Onc of the various senior purchase professionals while talking to me said that he likes his job for "The simple reason that he has to meet people who think that they can outsmart him", This one thing always keeps him on his toes and ever alert.

While meeting the sales people the PM also some how finds time for

1. Vendor development
2. Inventory control/ stores management
3. Ordering
4. Purchases at the peak capacities and at the slow down
5. Credit control for the suppliers
6. Deciding correct quantity, quality, price, delivery schedules, contracts. Transports, sourcing both internal and external, and the most important the payment terms favouring the company.

Depending upon the inputs from my colleagues we can have following types of PMs.

1. Those who listen
2. Those who do not listen.
3. Those who know what they want exactly.
4. Those who try to get the best deals.
5. Those who show that they are very open.
6. Those who go by rules
7. Those who bend and break here and there. But are honest.
8. Those who appreciate sales and the efforts going in
9. Those who are straight forward and knowledgeable.
10. Those who are corrupt.

You would say that all sorts are covered here, may be yes or no. they are just like other human beings, but probably overstressed due to factors outside their control. Moreover, purchase is a staff function so other functions like production, finance, marketing try to treat them like not so important and also like a readymade punching bag.

The sales people are absolutely incomplete without this vital factor in the process called selling.

Purchase managers are more relevant in the industrial marketing. There is no dearth of experts in the industry. Steel, cement, power, coalfields and such sectors have many. Every salesman learns a lot from these almost wizards. There are a few who may not buy from you but even then, they teach you a thing or two. They can discuss why the orders were not placed on you. It is suggested that the salesman must find suitable time to discuss things with the PM. He may earn a lot more than many trainings combined at his company.

PMs have little time for incompetence. They inadvertently turn into cynics as they are constantly aware of the threat of getting cheated. Though the functions of the PM remain somewhat similar in all sectors, each sector needs a special expertise to cater to the demanding and exact needs of the production and other departments.

***

CHAPTER SIX

INTERNAL SELLING

INTERNAL SELLING

Internal selling is not a very common term and even the fresh sales people are not aware about this very peculiar phenomenon. The salesman encounters internal selling once he starts getting orders. Every salesman has suffered due to this many times self-destructive process, which has potential to destroy the developed market for a company. Generally, nobody is careful enough and hence this dirty process with office politics as a supplement is thriving in every company. To understand this peculiar process, we have to go back to the beginning of the salesman's career. After the usual training, and few days of rest-in period the salesman goes in the market with the sole purpose of getting orders. He discovers that whatever training he had been given is inadequate. The market is ruthless and it teaches the real selling. He faces a tremendous pressure from the bosses for completion of the targets, and coverage of area. He somehow finds ways to find, talk, and get orders. Overjoyed he very innocently forwards or submits the orders to the branch or head office, and expects some really smooth processing. Here he faces yet another unexpected and very stark reality which is called the "internal selling"

He is not at all prepared or equipped for this shock. More often than not he finds that the external selling to outside customers is easy when compared to internal selling.

The salesman has a fair idea about the delivery schedules, costs, and accordingly he commits to the customer. Suddenly he finds that the people who should have been on his side are acting very strange and many times he feels like he is an outsider.

Why this happens?

How many sales managers are aware about such a problem in their organizations? If they know what all they do about the same? They have an organization to cope up with diverse issues. They must weigh much more than the lonely salesman.

Internal Selling

Internal Selling

Once the processing office receives the order it is marked to a department called sales administration department (SAD). The department checks out the order for the discrepancies and other things. It formally accepts or rejects the order. When the order is accepted, an acknowledgement is sent to the party along with tentative delivery schedules. The order is then forwarded to the production department. They produce either fresh goods or supply from the existing stocks. The packed and finished goods are handed over to the despatch department.

In the meanwhile, the accounts department raises the invoice and transporters details are included and the goods are finally despatched. The salesman then collects payments and one cycle of sales is completed. Very simple, isn't it? We should never have any problems in such a simple and clean process. But you would know that even the very simple things when done on a large scale, many times can become messy.

Today one of my friends who is working in a office furniture products company, very *reputed at that*, narrated a very interesting story to me. His monthly target was Rs. Nine lakhs and the quarterly (April May June) target was Rs. twenty-seven lakhs. He placed an order worth six lakhs and thirty-eight thousand and his target was achieved on 15th June itself. He was already in the extra five percent and was making plans for spending the extra money.

At this point, the regional manager walked in the office and the trouble started for my friend. Out of the item for he had collected nearly forty percent were out of stock with no chance of getting them on the assembly line for at least next ten weeks. The regional manager with all his polish and smooth talk and of course, his ever-present laptop had nothing good to say. Further he said that the company would be able to supply only chairs but not the tables for next ten weeks.

My friend was absolutely crest fallen. But he was of the older seasoned stock of hardcore salesman, he reconciled very fast. He got the present stock list. Proceeded to the client and somehow could negotiate for the terms and at the end of the month could still get his extra 5%. Any experienced sales person would be able to identify himself with my friend.

The problem with Indian management is that the influence of the people in the factory or the H/O is exaggerated. In many companies the peon of the MD is more powerful than the managers. The production people have no feeling for what goes on in the market. Ask any production manager, he would always tell that his products are world class, and simply because of this *sole reason* they should be automatically sold. Very strange! The efforts of the production are very visible because of the piling of stocks and because of the money invested. And more often than not they are in daily touch and within hearing distances of the decision-making-unit of the organisation.

As against the salesman is in some god forsaken place doing his best to sell the "World-class" products. He is doing his best but has no witness to bear him out. He is working against all odds. He gets the orders. The effort most likely goes unappreciated, after all the products are world class.

So, when he gets some problems, he has to initiate a process called as Internal selling. As earlier explained, there are many pitfalls between the procurement of the order and getting paid for same.

<u>Sales Administration Department</u>

The acronym for this dept. is very appropriately SAD. Generally, the people here are working overtime to show that they are working. Maybe they are! Let us assume, that a company is getting about hundred orders per day. So, each of the members has his work cut out. The time study shows that each order takes about ten minutes to process. So, you can calculate the load etc. But unfortunately for the salesman they work in the visibility of the marketing managers and they can create an impression that they are the busiest people in the office if not the city. They behave as if each order they process is their own and the salesman is not involved. All salesmen are facing the tussle with the SAD day in and day out.

The usual reasons thrown at the face of the salesman are:

1. Order is not clear.
2. Stocks not available
3. Raw material shortage
4. Order confirmation not received from the party.
5. Power cuts
6. Labour problems
7. Transporter does not accept the consignments.
8. Sanctions from MD for the rates offered cannot be taken as MD is out of country
9. Payment terms not acceptable.

The salesman is involved in convincing /or selling the importance of fulfilling the order. He talks about the importance of the order in the overall plans of the company. He cajoles, deals with soft hands but sometimes he has to threaten to contact the MM or MD. This is a routine affair in the lives of salesmen.

After all this the order somehow reaches the production plant. In the normal times the order gets supplied. But in about thirty percent times the complications set in. the reasons cited are:

1. Production scheduling (or lack of it)
2. Power shortages
3. Lack of manpower
4. Lack of one component, rest everything is available
5. Sometimes sheer callous indifference
6. Apart from the salesman no body in the company is happy for the increase in orders. They see it as additional load.

Let us assume that the order has been supplied and the client rejects the goods on the basis of poor quality. This triggers a new war between salesman and the quality control people. The general attitude of the Q/C people towards the salesman is poor to say the least.

To complicate the matters further if the product is so-called *technical* and the concerned salesman is so-called *non- technical,* then the qc manager takes a quick test on the product knowledge of the salesman on the phone or in person. Very grudgingly he accepts to test the product.

What an insult?

All this time the salesman is trying to cope up with the irritated, livid and wildly abusive customer. He is bound by the procedure in which he has to procure a sample from the customer, and fill in a detailed report. He sends the sample with a report and then the eternal waiting for the reply from the q/c. This is easy when the salesman and the plant is in the same state. But if the plant and the client are in two different states of India, then lot of paperwork is to be attended. This may take a week to a fortnight. By this time the customer is ready to kick the salesman.

After the due delay, a report is sent to the client.

Any guesses?

The report categorically states that the product sample was within the *tolerance limits, and that it conforms to BIS, DIN, ASTM* and a few others. The q/c has successfully washed away his hands. In no way the report helps the salesman and the heat is even more. Here he is with a questionable material firm his company and with a livid customer. Ask any salesman worth his salt he would have a very little good to say about the qc people. (There should be a comprehensive and integrated training in which the production and Q/C people must visit at least one client per month so that a lot of cobwebs would be cleared. Similarly, the sales people should also be made aware about production and Q/C process.)

One more department with whom the salesman has a continuous clash is the accounts and finance. These people behave even bigger than the boss himself. They think that they own the company and accordingly they treat the lesser mortals called salesmen.

Many times, I have tried to analyse the internal hot tussle and have been able to find out some possible solutions.

1. The salesman must be in constant touch with all these departments as his performance depends on their work culture.

2. **He must develop a solid rapport with these people. In fact, he must treat these people as the most important customers. Why? Simply because these are the people he is stuck up with. He cannot change them. If the**

salesman has some issues with the outside customers, he has a choice, he can find some new customer. He can work with them or dump them. In his own company he has no choice. What can he do?

3. Always carry gifts for the SAD/and production people.
4. Never step on the toes of even a peon in the head office. You never know he might be the only person when the boss had started the company.
5. Keep very good relations with the drivers, personal assistants, and such people of the MD, MM, or even the FM. They would give you the information which may save you and your job.
6. Develop your image as a good salesman and let people know that you mean business.
7. Pray to God that He gives them some insight of your job.

Once a friend of mine was negotiating a big deal with a government department. The direct demanding office was the DRM, the divisional railway manager. He was convinced about the products but as per their rules he needed a demo and samples at the site. So, he placed a trial order for small quantity, and after the usual checks the final orders would be placed. Please note no FREE samples! My friend was aware about the SAD in his company, and how callously they handle small quantity orders. So, he made a page long justification and further projection of the orders along with the formal order.

After a fortnight nothing happened. He got worried, he talked to SAD, they said that they had despatched the order. As a last resort he spoke to the MD and requested a fast response.

Two days later he received a long letter telling him that the address of the DRM Central Railway had changed and the *poor* courier could not locate the address. We all know that the offices of DRMs etc generally do not change and even if they do, the frequency would be once in a century.

My friend was at the end of his wits. He called the SAD who were protecting the courier as they were getting their money from the courier company. The salesman was on the last priority. He confirmed in writing that the DRM office was **"where it was"** but requested the SAD to send the parcel to his residential address. All this wasted about two more weeks, the order was lost. All because of some callously careless attitude of the SAD people. My friend was disgusted and he quit the company. But now he is more careful.

So, in short, all aspiring and practising salesmen must treat *internal selling* more important than the external selling. Any failure in internal selling can result in a loss of order, loss of face, or even a loss of job. The tussle between the procedure and the on-the-job field decisions would never end. They see the elephants in a different and personalised perspective. Salesman wants to bend some rule just for getting the long-awaited closing of an order. But his effort gains no ground unless the SAD understands the pain of what happens in selling. So far nothing much has changed so the battle is on.

***

CHAPTER SEVEN

PHILOSOPHY OF SALES

PHILOSOPHY OF SALES

I can already see that very wry smile on your face, as you read the heading of this chapter. You are probably saying to yourself "Come on! What has philosophy to do with sales?" Normally you would be right in saying so in cases of most of the sales people you might have interacted with. But I divide the sales fraternity into two categories as follows:

1. Those who sell because they like to
2. Those who sell because they do not have anything else to do.

In the present post pandemic scenario in our country we find that jobs are hard to come by, the VRS is shifting CRS, where contract employees are slowly but steadily replacing the regular on the roll employees, where many giants in public sector are facing distinct lockout possibilities, where the general atmosphere is a queer mixture of inflation and deflation, where the plum jobs are very rare, where for a job of a peon in a government postgraduates apply, were fresh graduates are mortally afraid to peep in to their future, where the size of Ascent supplement is all time small, where software professionals are queuing for normal menial jobs, the things look bleak.

In such a scenario, people after graduating find that getting a job in the sales field is comparatively easy. No exams, and no grind like the medical, engineering fields entry exams if one wants to start as a salesman. There is no restriction. Probably, because of an easy entry, most people enter this field without knowing much about the same. It is easy!

The entry point is the major reason for the success or failure in the sales job. Chances of people who succeed in this very unforgiving and trying career are higher in case it is a "Chosen" field. Those who fail are generally those, who enter sales as a second or even a third choice. In fact, this may be the demarcating factor between the better and the *bitter salesman.* The process of sales has to be understood and further if possible internalised.

The philosophy of sales can be better understood if the process of sales is properly studied.

What is Sales process?

Classically it is defined as a fair, equal, legal, exchange of goods or services to fulfil one's need or needs against some pre-decided compensation say in terms of money. And as per the real wizard and guru of modern marketing, Philip Kotler the marketing is the efforts put in to generate the repetitive sales of the same product to same or different consumers.

There is a tendency to use these two terms as same or equivalent or instead of each other which is totally wrong. Marketing is more comprehensive as well as integrated process of which sales is a function, albeit n important one.

Sales can survive without marketing but it is not vice versa.

So let us start at the basics:

- What do you do when you buy anything?
- What are the factors that make you buy a particular product?
- What is the impact of promotion in your purchase decision?
- What is the role of the opinions you receive from friends, or relatives?
- What is the role of price in the purchase decision?
- What is the part played by the person on the spot (point of purchase)?
- Are you really **sure** that you want to buy a particular product from a wide range of similar products available right in front of you? If *yes* why? Also,

if you are *sure*, are you *sure* for the reasons that make *you sure*?

As per my experience and understanding sale of any product is because of the confidence generated by the salesman for himself first and then for his product.

Let me try to explain by asking you a question!

How often you buy a product from a salesman you do not like or trust? Usual answer would be a NO. The product and its details, utility, after sales service, and even price would cross your mind much later and certainly after your acceptance of the salesman as a decent and sincere person. So, any sale is a direct or indirect reflection of this confidence.

There are three basic components (or more recently referred to as the stake holders) of the sales function.

1. The first and the foremost is you as the customer
2. The product you really want to buy to fulfil your perceived need
3. The person who offers services to provide you the product.

Let us analyse the first component is in some more details.

You: You decide whether the process would be initiated, continued and concluded by the actual payment of money.

So, take out "you" from the sales and the process turns futile without any real objective. Can you imagine playing a football match without a goal post? All twenty-two players and two referees cannot play football without the goalposts. Similarly, always remember that 'you' form the vital part of the process. At the same time, you alone cannot control the process. The reason is that you are one of the many customers. If you decide not to buy it hurts but there are more options. Someone else would buy. So, in such a case the salesman has to find a new house, another door or an organization who would have need for his product.

Product: When you buy a product you are fulfilling one of your many needs. Many times, that is why, even the best of salesmen cannot close a sale as the customer he is talking to is not interested in that product at that particular moment of time. There are two types of customers. The first type is the one who knows exactly what he wants and the second who does not know what is needed by him. The first is relatively easy to deal with. If you have the right product then it would be bought rather than sold at a full price. Second type would be slightly tricky. Here the salesman has to work a lot more. He has to identify the need, then suggest a solution, then recommend the product. The sales occur subsequently. Because the customer is in doubt he listens to all salesmen from all available companies and gets even more confused and lands up with a product that may not be at all suitable.

A simple advice for the customers as to how they should decide:

- Identify the need.
- Classify the need.
- Crystalise the need.
- Do a short cost benefits analysis on need versus the cost of fulfilling the need.
- Arrive at a conclusion.
- Then search for a brand.
- Then simply buy.

The person who tries to fulfil your need i.e., the salesman.:

Salesman is a person who most people underrateandunderestimate, or even ridicule. How often have you closed your door on the face of a salesman? Have you ever thought that in spite of all insults, derogation, ridicule how salesmen still achieve their goals or targets?

The logic is simple. A customer for any salesman is a number. The customer is a part of yes and no game. When a salesman is moving in the market following things would be more or less constant.

1. His target in numbers like so many pieces per month
2. Territory is constant.
3. Total number of available customers at any given point of time

So, what should he do? He has to find his averages. Suppose he finds that out each ten persons contacted two would buy his products. And his target is, say, 100. Then it simply means that he has to contact five hundred people. Now instead of finding out how he would find five hundred people if he starts analysing why eighty percent say no, he would be in a serious crisis. All he has to do is change the focus to those who say yes, and be happy for those who say yes. If he manages to focus on yes, he would be happier, would have better focus, and would have more chances of becoming successful and staying successful. Sales is a repetitive process and this fact should never be forgotten. It is the intent to work than intelligent to work which succeeds in sales.

Initially in this chapter we described two types of salesmen.

The first type which has people who sell because they like to sell and generally, they follow the proven and well-travelled path of more contacts result in more sales. They do it knowingly or inadvertently. They do their jobs with pleasure and a smile on their face.

The law of averages is for the second types who sell because they could not do anything else. And presently also they nothing else to do. If they inculcate the habit of following the rule of average and start to contact more people when it hurts them the most, they would start producing results. And believe me success is the biggest possible motivator.

Second important thing the salesman should always remember is to contact people with whom they do not feel comfortable. Most salesmen while away their precious time in chatting and gossiping chatting with the customers who make them comfortable. These customers may never buy the products and hence the salesman would categorise these calls as the follow -up calls in his daily sales reports. These calls are one of the root causes in the fall of performance. The supervisors who are smart insist that at least two new customers must be contacted on a daily basis. The logic in this is simple as any thing else in sales. As per the wise men 'If a product is exposed to a substantial sample of prospective buyers the sale of product would follow a set pattern of yes and no over a period of time.' The pattern would have variations and hence a smart supervisor is necessary. So, if a salesman knows and understands this rule, he is not likely to be discouraged by a barrage of '*no*' *es* in the market. But does this alone suffice? A big no!

The salesman has to essentially know and internalise following things.

1. Personal appearance.
2. Product knowledge.
3. Knowledge about the customers and their needs.
4. Complete trust in his ability and his products.
5. Act in genuine enthusiasm.
6. Know his own pattern of percentages of getting <u>a yes and a no.</u>

It can be safely concluded that if a salesman knows his customer fully, and is prepared to try out his percentage principle, he should find himself in more happy situations and should be able to maintain good posture.

The salesman should also know that the process of sales is and <u>equal exchange</u> between the need and the price. So ideally, he should not be begging for a sale. On the other hand, he has to also know that he has to be decent, humble and a facilitator to the customer. He must bear in his mind:

"For every customer, who does not buy from him, he can find an alternate customer, but so can every customer find an alternate product and a salesman in whom he can trust more."

Till such time a workable balance is maintained selling remains a funny and satisfying profession.

***

CHAPTER EIGHT

BOSS/BOSSES/ BOSSISM

Boss/ Bosses/ Bossism

In any field, one needs constant guidance and mentoring to remain on the right course and be productive as per the expectations of the management. It is accepted that without a mentor or a guru you are more likely to go down. **"Binguru Gyan kahan se pau"** very appropriately describes the relationship between a guru and a pupil.

While we acquire our education many teachers, guides, mentors and coaches form us from outside and from inside. During this stage, the person is young and immature so he rarely understands the effort that goes in. The proverbial putty is being shaped by many sculptors. When the formal education is over (and done with) one starts to think and work about his career one absolute fact surfaces. It tells him that whatever knowledge he gained is a mere gate pass to an enormous arena called "life". In a professional life whether one is successful or not, greatly would depend upon what sort of boss he gets in his first job. You may talk to many successful people in diverse professions and would find one common thing that they all had a boss who taught them right things, in a right way and at right times. The initial stage becomes the solid foundation for a successful life.

Let us understand this special person, with whom every body has to interact. One has to be alert in his presence, listen to him with rapt attention and even keep him happy and perform as per his expectations.

Boss to me is a **"Better Organised Superior Soul"**. We try to describe an ideal boss. An ideal boss for whom the juniors are ready stretch beyond limits or more fashionably stop a bullet for him. If you have such a person to work, most of your problems do not even germinate. So, you start thinking about the attributes of a person for whom you would willingly stop a bullet. What is the first that comes to your mind, the second or the third and so on and so forth.

1. That he should be a good human being. Think about this for a while. A good human being is available almost everywhere, but not all of them cannot be good bosses. But this is the first thing that comes to our mind. Though it is not enough by itself.
2. That he should be knowledgeable.
3. That he should know where he is going
4. That he should be sincere and not a phoney.
5. That he should be a team-man'.
6. That he should be approachable.
7. That he should be balanced
8. That he should not be a credit monger
9. That he should be fair to all involved.
10. That he should be strict but he should give a fair trial to a person failing in his initial tasks
11. Absolute sound character as far as money and women are concerned.
12. That he should be able **to do**, what you are supposed to do, in a much better way than you.
13. Lastly, he must be a "Practise first preach later".

You may add your own as this list is not complete. When your list is ready try to rate your present boss on a scale of one to ten and if possible, show it to him and watch his response and his behaviour later on. This single thing would tell you many things about him.

During my entire career, I met only one person who used to give us a format called "Boss Appraisal Format". He had a tabulated format where in we were just supposed to tick. More surprisingly, the corrections suggested were adopted by this wonderful Person.

The discussion here should be enough to give you an idea about what an ideal boss should be. The further part would tell you what you would find in the practical future life of a salesman.

So, a classification is offered:

1. **Let us do it type:** this type of the bosses is highly educated, very sober, and believe in delegating. They know exactly what they want, and more often than not, have even the roles written for their junior colleagues. They would help quite a few times if you are sincerely putting in the efforts.

2. **Phoney over-dressed type:** Usually you would come across this type in advertisements or white goods sector. They can be good but the percentages are more towards the worse. They are more concerned about their looks than the products or the market. Generally, they are not very well received. The market responds in its own inimitable way, which means that they are ridiculed. If you are not sure about whether a person is a phoney or not all you have to do is to watch their eyes. Their smile hardly ever reaches their eyes. They would never remember anything you told them. They would over

react and put all the blames on you that too in front of the dealers or customers. They would promise things which they you know can never be fulfilled. They have a lens ready to find faults in everything and everyone around them. If you are in a town and he is from a metro then you would listen to the insufficiencies hundred times in one day. One such person used to be my boss.He was a pain everywhere. When he came to Nagpur (which is a fairly big city, 10th largest in India) we were having a lunch, in a three-star ITDC approved restaurant. He dissected each dish to such a level that I lost all my appetite. He ate everything on the course, but he compared and complained about everything. He also told me "See if you have to have a chicken clear soup nothing beats Sheraton, sizzlers only in Kolkata, and fish only in Amritsar." I thanked God that this fellow was not working internationally. A thought crossed my mind. If this fellow would be half as fastidious towards the job as he was for his food our company would be making double the sales and the profit. But then he was the boss!

3. **English only type:** This type is a sure disaster if you are working in company which caters to rural markets in India. In quite a few markets in UP, MP, Maharashtra, and even in Gujrat the dealers hardly give any response leave aside positive to English. At the back of such bosses there is a constant funny commentary going on. The worse part is their English as a language is very limited. They speak with horrible accents and their written communication is pathetic. To tackle this type, you have to be diplomatic enough to tell him that the dealers are not as good as him so he should speak in Hindi or the local language.

4. **Amateur Psychologists type:** This is one of deadliest species of the bosses. Because if they conclude that you are not their type your career in that company is over. Be very careful of how you behave in front of these people.

    For example

    - If you laugh a lot - You are casual.
    - If you talk a little loudly - you are arrogant.
    - If you sit resting in the

    back of a chair - You are laid back.

    - If you cross your hands - You are negative
    - If you wear dark shirts - You have criminal tendencies

    It goes on and on...

It is really surprising that these people easily condemn good, decent, hard -working people for them. Even Sigmund Freud would have been more careful about such statements, but not these people. These people are overly interested in the family background of a person. If they come to know that some person five generations ago had some minor issues, they would immediately start looking for symptoms in your behaviour. All your accomplishments have no bearing. It would help this type to read in depth about body language, kinesics, and psychology before hanging their people.

The first thing a student of psychology learns is not to study any behavioural pattern is absolute isolation. There are simpler explanations available for actions of people than the phobia, mania, and psychosis.

1. **Bulldozer Divers:** This is the most common type in the Indian scenario. They would shout, scream and always ready to throw a tantrum at you asking you to do what nobody has done from the inception of the company. They expect you to do but if you ask for how they would not know. Very loud both in appearance and sound. You have to develop your own discounting factors when you deal with such a boss. If you are keen and observant enough you would talk to your seniors and find out whether he is a barking or a biting boss.

2. **All are fools in this company:** This type is usually available in the regional or zonal offices of the companies. These would constantly tell their juniors about how he improved the lots in the company by confronting the MD or even better the chairman and telling them the mistakes in the company. You better do not believe him until you see the truth in the all India/ national level meetings. Here you would notice that nobody in the top management ever notice him. You would further observe that he would accept everything the top boss says and that he would contradict everything he promised you and he would stop at nothing in becoming the best available_stainless-steel spoon_ in the meeting.

3. **All core no polish:** These types are generally available on the shop floor type industries. These people are simply superb. They would anything to meet the targets. They know their team very well. They fight for their people and the management knows that this is a _real man_ who is not bothered about anything except the core work. They get a lot of respect. People look up to them. All organizations should treat them as the real assets. I have seen a few of this type. Even today I wonder how

they produced without a blemish and met the deadlines without any failures. You would rarely see such a person in the comforts of AC. You would find him toiling with the machines and with grease on his hands.

4. **When I was in States/ Europe/ Japan type:** There are plenty of this type in today's situations. They begin and end with their monotonous routine.

"In States they do it in this way. Here it is rubbish." They would ask for everything but would rarely achieve anything worthwhile. If caught with this type you take a deep breath and bear somehow and sincerely wish to God to send these people back to where they came from.

9. **Appreciative:** This is a rare commodity. Probably most conventional bosses believe that any appreciation reduces the zeal to work. They have never believed that a simple pat on the back can double the output. "You did a good job, keep it up" is the real energy for the people in the organization. Like all good things the appreciative boss is also very rare almost like a black pearl.

10. **Cool as a cucumber type:** This is also a rare type. But not as rare as the previous one. They have a way of absorbing shocks, which is contagious and works very well for the team. In times of distress and duress they would simply say "Okay, forget what has happened. Let us concentrate on the future. What can we really do now? Do you need any special approvals etc? in the long run they always finish the race with flying colours. Not only that they also create a strong team.

I hope you have a fair idea of what you would be getting in your jobs. The list can be further stretched, but that would redundant.

One story would explain the behaviours and what can be waiting for you.

In one of the companies, I worked a funny situation developed. Three bosses converged on me as I was the number two. One was a regional manager; one was the out going branch manager and the third was the incoming branch manager.

As usual at the behest of the RM it was decided that an announcement of the change in management would be made by him at the dealer cum press conference. I was told to arrange the same. Time was 2 PM! Somehow by seven thirty in the evening everything was arranged. A special venue, preparation at the venue, power point presentation was ready. It went very well and the dealers and press went home happy.

The actual fun started after the event. I was shocked when the RM told me that press release must have only his photo with the information. The outgoing BM came and told me that he alone is important and only he should appear in the photographs. The incoming BM who would be my immediate boss for the next few years was even more candid. He told me that photograph should naturally include him alone. I knew that I was in a hopeless situation. I was thinking furiously but nothing seemed worthwhile.

Then suddenly a flash came to my mind. I asked my photographer friend to take a professional snap of the new model to be launched, along with flowers in the background. That was the only photograph which appeared in the press release. And nobody could complain. I could hardly believe that the senior as in designation and age could be so petty minded. It was big lesson for me and I learnt *how not to behave* as a manager.

Bossism: One very interestingconcept one must understand if one has to survive, grow and reach the top of the ladder in Indian management scenario. For that matter in anything and anywhere in the world. The concept of bossism!

There are many perceptions going around when you utter the word boss. The most popular one is the one poster saying "The boss is always right". Everybody except the boss enjoyed the monkey in the poster. You must have seen the one if not then just go to nearest Archies gallery and see.

Is the boss always, right? If he is or he is not? Does it really matter?

Seemingly, the boss is always right matters, because the concept of bossism originates here. The worst part is further that most bosses seriously believe in this statement. If are an operating boss you may not answer to me but you may in your mind answer.

Bossism is more prominent in the government or public sector. Ask any executive engineer or a plant manager he would tell you incredible, as well as bizarre stories. They have to cope up with their bosses doing many things outside the purview of their job profile. As if the bosses are not enough their wives are added as a bonus. If your plant in Banaras, guess what is most liked by the lady and the lord! A silk saree to begin with, a VIP darshan, boat rides, and so many other things. Same story can happen in Mumbai, Pune, Hyderabad, and almost all cities. Average expenses can run in to thousands of rupees and even then, the boss and *his boss* are not satisfied.

You can see many scenes at the airport where, the garlands, the bottles, the fake smiles, the extra humility, and the hidden disgust tell the inside story. Are they acceptable, funny or sickening?

One simple theory about the boss! If the boss has to tell that he is the boss then he is not. He may be a mere senior person because he was born earlier than you. He may be a person seating in the chair by fluke. In the minds of his employees, he is simply a nuisance and a professional evil which has to be tolerated.

Does it mean that all bosses are either good or bad? No, it would not be black or white but more in grey shade. And as it goes in the other activities of life statistics takes over. No boss can be the ideal variety. He may have some good, some acceptable qualities. On the other side of spectrum, he may have some shortcomings. Also, various situations would affect his performance. You can always rate him on a scale of 1 to10, and derive your own conclusions. Best way to do is to imagine that you are the boss. Mentally seat in his chair try to think like him. Most of the things would be sorted out by asking simple questions and finding solutions. Many times, you would be surprised that how close you are to him in the thinking.

Getting a good boss is as important like getting a good wife or husband. In both cases, adjustments and flexibility are needed. One who adjusts faster benefits faster in both cases. A man has to accept that he works with two bosses. The boss at the workplace may turn out as a less dangerous option as you can change him by changing the job. So, enjoy at both places while you can.

As a person from marketing, I would always prefer a boss who has some basic understanding in front line selling. You would be surprised the ease with which you can work with such a person. He would be sympathetic, and strict but he would stand by you. Ask any active sales person "What frustrates you most?" very often he would tell like debriefing to a non-sales boss. One of them told me that *non sales and nonsense* go hand in hand.

So far, we have tried to describe and analyse the very significant part in the organization.

One more story relating to a *Number One* man in one of the largest companies in India, now expanding very fast in States and Europe.

He is a middle-aged restless man, very graceful, soft spoken and generally believing himself and his people. Guess what does he do on a daily basis? In his huge chamber which has a round table and few chairs, he has a routine. The room is at the top floor and has full glass on one side. He has a recliner called in Hindi as *aaramkhurchi*. He seats in this chair playing with ideas, notions, concepts and possibilities. He says that he lives in the future. At least ten years ahead, and visualises what his company would look like, work like, in the future. He likes to paint the future with all possible colours. He is at peace and at his creative best when he in in the chair.

When an idea is germinated, he would call all relevant stakeholders, and have a brainstorming session. No bars type. Many ideas were a waste of time but quite a few finally got converted and still evolving which makes this as the brand leader and social leader. Most certainly and importantly it is not the end but just a plain milestone in a well-planned journey.

Do you think your boss resembles to the described version in any single way? If yes, consider yourself, as the lucky one. Very... very lucky at that!

Please remember that even if you know all the interesting information about your boss it does not actually help you. Between you and your boss it is always you who would have to change, adjust, alter, edit and ensure that you stay in the organization. you have to find the golden mean, where you are more acceptable to your boss. Rest everything including the customers, market come a distant second. As today most organisations select very average workers, who have lesser skills but are more prone to take things lying down.

You would be well placed if you learn from each of your bosses what should be done and what should not be done. At least in the future your staff would be happy.

***

CHAPTER NINE

LIFE TIME TIPS FOR SALESMEN

Life time tips for salesmen

1) Check list for a professional salesman

Every salesman should check for the following in his bag and /or laptop.

1. **Office stationery.**

- Large letterheads
- Small letterheads
- Continuation sheets
- Order booking and order confirmation formats
- Quotations formats
- Envelopes small and large
- Product literatures preferably a file
- Product price lists
- Comparison of his products with the nearest competitors
- Certifications like BIS/IS/ ASTM etc
- Important order copies for references.
- Product manuals
- Authority letters if any required

- Identity papers
- Rough pads
- His diary
- Receipt books
- Income tax clearance certificates

1. **<u>Office accessories</u>**

- Pens blue /black / red
- Stapler with pins
- Small 6 inches' scale
- Calculator
- Cello tape
- Gum bottle or tube
- Sealing wax
- Candle with match box
- Company seal if required for sealing quotations
- Postage stamps/ E-mail IDs/ fax numbers
- Revenue stamps for pre-receipts
- Circular stamp of the company

3. **<u>General</u>**

- Railway time table/airlines schedules
- City maps if visiting a new city
- Medicine box he should be aware of his needs. Usually anti allergents, medicine for headaches, common cold, stomach upsets. Actually, you should get a proper advice from your family doctor and as per the same the emergency kit must be prepared. A working day lost due to bad health can be very costly.

4. **<u>Credit cards and cash</u>**

The idea is simple. You should never come back to your office for collecting something which you ought to have in the first place as a regular item in your bag.

***

2.Diary

As earlier mentioned in this book your habit of maintaining a diary or not can create a run of the mill salesman or an extraordinary one. Diary is a habit which a few lucky ones naturally have but most have to acquire the same. Chronological listing of whatever happens around you can empower you. Also, it is admissible as evidence in the court of law.

It is suggested that any salesman who is serious and committed to his job MUST never retire for the day before he enters his day in the diary. It would never take more than fifteen minutes- *if you maintain on a daily basis*- to finish this task. As in the case of all small and avoidable chores it is very tempting to postpone it for tomorrow, which never comes. Even a single day delay can make it go for ever. The power comes from the regularity of the habit and not from you actually write. You may miss a point or two but it does not matter, as is covered in next few days.

Once you decide to write a diary you should better learn to writing it effectively. After a lot of trial and errors a format is suggested. But it is not the best. You should customise for your own needs.

1. **Inside cover page (First):** All addresses/ mobile numbers with codes/ Emails/ details of Head Office and other offices. Residence numbers of your colleagues. Your emergency numbers.
2. **Inside cover page (last):** All telephone numbers of your clients, dealers, professionals, professionals,

newspapers, ad agencies and even friends and advocates.

Your diary should be in such a way that when you refer to it the person in front should accept what you say. It should be a record you can trust.

Sample page from diary

Sample page from diary

Place:
Date:
Day:

Appointment	Discuss with
1.	1. Name: Matter
2.	2.
3.	3.
4.	4.
5.	5.
	Do not Forget

1.   Last date of Tenders etc.
2.   Monthly meeting
3.   Air   sales   service promises
4.
5.

Telephone to	Attend Matters On
1.	1.
2.	2.
3.	
Today's Events	Matters Brought
& Personal Notes:	Forward to:

New Contacts Made
(Very important as it creates new business)
New Referrals   1.
    2.

Summary

Today's Sale
Cumulative Sale:
Today's Collection:
Cumulative Collection:

Ideal Page Of Sales Diary

3)SHORT AND SWEET

PLEASE remember following forever:

- Bank accepts **only** cash /cheques/ demand drafts/ NEFT / RTGS
- Projection of sales is a tool **not money**.
- How many **new** customers you contacted today?
- Have you asked for any **referrals**?
- Analyse the order before celebrations. Are **you making any Money?**
- We do business for **earning profits.**

Who is a satisfied customer?

He buys again and again. Repeats orders.

Buys other products of the company.

Talks favourably to Ohers about you, your products and about your company.

Pays less attention to competitor's advertisements and promotions.

Simple but most effective report

Today's sale =

Cumulative sales =

Today's collection =

Cumulative collection =

Rest everything is an effort to accomplish the above.

Things you should always remember as a salesman

1. You are not the only one who thinks smart. There are many others. More so in your own category of products and services.
2. If the order value is more never go alone. Always hunt in pairs.
3. Always listen first. Let the customer talk as he knows the best about what he wants.

4. Try to be different than the typical boring salesman.

5. Prepare yourself, separately for each individual customer. Till it becomes a habit.

6. See things. Ambience around the customer can tell you much more than what he actually tells you.

7. Ease the customer into a need.

8. Be clear, concise and correct.

9. Use pause. Never prompt any action. Never hurry him for taking a decision. Never ever say 'It is a tough time etc'

10. Never restart your sales discussion or pitch once you have reached the closing stage.

11. Always ask for money.

12. You put value on your products. If you feel they are worthy or worthless then they are.

13. Appear sincere, knowledgeable, and straight forward.

14. Do not give an "over smart" or a stuffy impression to your customer.

15. In some product lines you need a partner. Always hunt in pairs. If your partner complements you, you have a better chance to be more successful.

***

9 798886 295641